SCHOOL

CLASSROOM

STUDIES

Volume Tw_____together

BY HELEN COWIE AND JEAN RUDDUCK

PUBLISHED BY BP EDUCATIONAL SERVICE
on behalf of the Co-operative Group Work Project,
Division of Education, University of Sheffield.

School and Classroom Studies is volume 2 of
"Learning Together Working Together," published
by BP Educational Service on behalf of the
Co-operative Group Work Project at Sheffield
University.

© BP International Limited 1988, Helen Cowie and
Jean Rudduck

First published 1988

350438

ISBN 0 86165 146 4

BP Educational Service, Britannic House, Moor Lane,
London EC2Y 9BU.

Designed by Keith Moss Design Associates

Typeset and Printed by Quorn Selective Repro Ltd,
Loughborough, Leics.

PREFACE

The co-operative group work project, *Learning Together, Working Together*, was funded by British Petroleum (BP) for four years, from 1985–87 (phase 1) and 1987–89 (phase 2).

In phase 1 we concentrated on trying to understand where group work was being used in schools and what teachers and pupils thought about it. We interviewed 162 teachers and over 100 pupils, we observed in classrooms, and we conducted studies of group work in four comprehensive schools. Since much of the support for group work as a way of learning was coming from industry, we also interviewed employers in the region to find out what their view of group work was.

In phase 2 of the project, we made a study of GCSE and the opportunities for co-operative group work which it is encouraging. We collaborated with teachers who wanted to establish situations in which pupils evaluate their own experiences of learning and working together. We tried out, in a secondary school, the idea, taken from industry, of the 'quality circle'. We ran in-service activities for teachers about the introduction and development of co-operative group work strategies in the class room.

The project has been managed by a team of people from the Division of Education, University of Sheffield: Dr Helen Cowie, Mrs Brenda Finney (Project Secretary) and Professor Jean Rudduck. The team would like to thank all the people who have worked with them during the first two years of the project. Our thanks go to all the teachers and pupils in schools in the region who spent time talking to us and allowing us to observe their work. We should also like to thank BP for the constant interest and support they have shown. And we should like to thank people from industry, business and commerce who have expressed their support for education by giving time to talking with us about group work.

CONTENTS

1 School Studies

2 Classroom Studies

SCHOOL AND CLASSROOM STUDIES

When and if we pass beyond the unspoken despair in which we are now living, when we feel we are again able to control the race to destruction, a new breed of developmental theory is likely to arise. It will be motivated by the question of how to create a new generation that can prevent the world from dissolving into chaos and destroying itself. I think that its central technical concern will be how to create in the young an appreciation of the fact that many worlds are possible, that meaning and reality are created and not discovered, that negotiation is the art of constructing new meanings by which individuals can regulate their relations with each other. It will not, I think, be an image of human development that locates all of the sources of change inside the individual, the solo child. For if we have learned anything from the dark passage in history through which we are now moving it is that man, surely, is not "an island, entire of itself" but a part of the culture that he inherits and then recreates. The power to recreate reality, to reinvent culture, we will come to recognize, is where a theory of development must begin its discussion of mind. (Bruner, 1986, p. 149)

1

SCHOOL STUDIES

INTRODUCTION

In this section we offer accounts of some of the ways in which different comprehensive schools have come to develop group work. The factors that account for the differences include such things as the school's history, its public image, its curriculum structures, its criteria for success, its opportunity for staff dialogue, and the commitment and power of individual teachers or groups of teachers. The accounts provide some interesting insights into the processes of institutional change. We have produced these accounts because we think that teachers are often interested in hearing about what goes on in other settings. As a teacher in one of the four schools said:

"We've moved away from the need to have kids sat
silently, working independently, which had been the traditionally
accepted view of how things were taught. We know more
about how kids learn, how they enjoy their work and so
on, but there seems to me a worrying factor that none of these
developments are really thoroughly explained
anywhere in the market place. No-one actually knows
what goes on in schools."

The studies are made available in part as a response to this teacher's plea. The studies are also interesting because they reveal how, even in such different settings, teachers express similar concerns and show similar patterns of perception.

The studies are based on interviews with individual teachers or groups of teachers in each school. We also talked with pupils and in two schools observed work in classrooms. In each case the studies, in draft form, were returned to the schools for comment and correction and for permission to include in this series.

While there is some similarity of view and experience the school studies also tell interestingly different stories. We have tried to characterise the main differences in the titles:

School A – The Atkin School:
A School at the Crossroads

School B – The Brightwood School:
Room at the Top?

School C – The Clayton School:
Beginning to grow!

School D – The Dale School:
Co-operating teachers, co-operating pupils

THE ATKIN SCHOOL: A SCHOOL AT THE CROSSROADS

The study is based on transcripts of interviews conducted with 22 of the school's staff. The interviews lasted about 20 minutes each. The Head teacher was interviewed at greater length. Two teachers also took part, with the Head, in a group discussion during our first visit to the school.

Interviews were held with: the Head Teacher; a Deputy Head; the Head of Middle School; the Director of Studies; the Head of Sixth Form; one teacher in charge of special needs; one maths teacher; two science teachers; four languages teachers; two English teachers; one Drama teacher; two History teachers; two Geography teachers; one design teacher, one Home and Community teacher. The Head was asked as far as possible to include in the list of teachers selected for interview some teachers whom he thought might be opposed to group work, some whom he thought might be strongly supportive of it, and some whom he thought might not have strong views. In our view, the Head identified staff who met these criteria. No member of staff, as far as we know, declined to be interviewed.

Background

"This is a grammar school turned comprehensive".

Carnley is a small, inland market town. It has two comprehensive schools. The Atkin School became a comprehensive in 1976 through the amalgamation of the boys' grammar school, established in 1669, and the girls' grammar school. The then Head of the boys' grammar school became the first Head of the comprehensive, and the present Head joined in 1978. Atkin School now shares its 6th form with the neighbouring comprehensive school which was formed out of the old boys' and girls' secondary modern schools.

The Atkin School has, since the arrival of the present Head, introduced BTec exams, City & Guilds 365 exams, CPVE work, a DUBS Enterprise Scheme (Durham University Business School) which the Head hopes will be developed throughout the fourth and fifth years, and strong links with local employers. It has recently won an RSA award for its work with three local employers: Falcon Bicycles, British Steel and British Rail.

Active tutorial work has been tried out and Nuffield Science was introduced and is now used selectively. The Head is keen to develop the school's links with the community, and many staff now feel it proper that more time and effort be devoted to this goal. The school has a very good reputation for examination results and the Head is concerned to publicize such achievements. At the same time he and his colleagues express concern lest, because of the school's past image, examination results are seen as the only indicator of the school's success and their growing links with industry and the community ignored.

There are at present 715 pupils on roll. Last academic year 119 pupils left after the end of the fifth year; 68 (36% of the fifth year) went into the sixth form.

The steel industry as a source of employment is in decline. Some school leavers are taken on by local firms; others go to the Technical College or into YTS. Unemployment is running at approximately 19% in the region (1987). Carnley is somewhat isolated and transport problems could deter young people from seeking jobs – if they existed – within normal commuting range. Employment tends therefore to be sought locally, but few youngsters, it seems, are "left high and dry".

Within the school, first year pupils work in mixed ability groups. Thereafter they are divided into two broad ability bands, with narrow setting for maths and languages. Pupils who are deemed to have special educational needs are withdrawn to work as a special class until they have made sufficient progress to be reintegrated, but they do join their peers for tutor group meetings.

The school has a uniform but it is "a bit of a struggle" to enforce it beyond the third year when the first set of uniforms has worn out!

Many of the staff who used to teach in the former boys' and girls' grammar schools are still in post and they acknowledge their traditional roots. Colleagues seem to get on well with each other and tolerate each others' differences where differences are apparent. There is no concerted push for change and yet many individuals believe that the school should change. The challenge is to reconcile the strengths of the past with the needs of the future. There is anxiety, for instance, that intake numbers are dropping and some teachers fear that parents may be beginning to think that if exam results don't secure jobs then schools ought to be concentrating as much on personal and social skills, an area which is well-developed in the curriculum of other neighbouring comprehensive schools which had their roots in the secondary modern tradition. The dilemma facing the Atkin school was clearly expressed by one teacher:

"Ought we to be putting our priorities in the citizen rather than someone with so many GCSEs and A levels?" (T5)

Group work

During the interviews, teachers were facing the situation – common enough in secondary schools – that they did not really know how their colleagues taught, sometimes even in their own department:

"I don't know about other subjects because we all work in our own little vacuum. We very rarely discuss exactly what we do. I think we just do our own thing really and hope we come out OK." (T13)

Asked where in the school they thought group work might be used, teachers invariably reply "in English" or "in Drama". The reasons offered reveal some interesting assumptions:

"People like the English staff can do group work. They're used to a large oral element in the 16+ exams ... In fact the very essence of the course is that they haven't got a body of facts." (T2)

"English because English is ... They can discuss it I suppose ... The English people will themselves argue that argument is good ... And to express yourself is good. Yes. Certainly." (T12)

"Well certainly in Drama - you couldn't do anything else I don't think ... I don't see how you can do Drama any other way (ie without pupils talking)." (T11)

Although teachers tend to say that group work is more likely to go on in English than anywhere else, most *are* doing some group work, although they admit to being uncertain whether what they do 'counts'. Usually it's an occasional activity, perhaps once or twice a term, or, if more regular, used for a short time each week to provide some variety in a single or double lesson.

An English teacher (T14) invites pupils to take some 30 lines of a text, write out some questions and answers based on the text, and then exchange questions and, later, answers with another group. The experience of mutual assessment is one that this teacher rates highly. Geographers use group work on field trips and one geography teacher (T20) also uses group work in class to help pupils explore social situations which are characterised by conflict or controversy. For instance, each group might represent different members of a community which is confronting a crisis that affects them in different ways. The groups use the evidence available and discuss the situation from the perspective of the role they have been asked to take.

A history teacher encourages non-examination pupils to do collaborative 'illustrative' work where pupils apply knowledge or test out the gaps in their knowledge by constructing models of buildings, events or systems. (T17) Another history teacher (T18) uses group work for role play and simulation activities. A maths teacher (T9) has prepared problem-solving packages which will support group activity. Modern languages teachers (T10 and T11) use group work for language practice, but only in situations where the teacher can offer a general framework within which the groups can work:

"You suggest a certain situation – they've got to learn a certain number of phrases and you say 'Right now. You have just learned to say "I would like to buy an ice cream and I would like strawberry flavour"'. Change the flavour of the ice cream, change the price and so on and it works." (T11)

There may be some bad pronunciation which the teacher can't monitor, "but on the other hand they're building up their confidence." The home economists work in groups most of the time and the room is of course designed with peninsular tables that seat four. The design teacher feels that in his subject pupils tend to work as individuals as the work becomes more advanced but he feels that there is still opportunity for criticism, in pairs or groups, of each other's products. Whereas most teachers use discussion in groups as a way of tackling the learning task, the chemistry teacher values paired work because it provides an opportunity for social chat while some fairly routine but necessary procedures are carried out:

"Now the nice thing about Chemistry is you sit and talk
to your friend. If you're filtering half a test tube of solution it
takes x minutes, and therefore what do you do in the x minutes?
As far as I'm concerned you can talk about anything you like.
It's a nice peaceful sort of life and I think that two people can
sit and talk about things they enjoy." (T8)

But the paired discussion in Chemistry can also be task-oriented:

"They can actually sit and discuss the work. If you're on
your own you haven't the opportunity to discuss what's going on
and sometimes you can miss things." (T8)

Another science teacher (T7) believes that such discussion is crucial and is what makes the difference between learning to be a chemist and merely 'doing' chemistry.

The interesting thing about the Atkin School is that much more group work is actually going on than people realize. But group work, as in most schools, is not perceived as part of the school's *corporate* teaching strategy. There are many reasons for this. One is that predominantly instructional teaching has been equated with academic success in examinations:

"I think that society tends to expect qualifications, and
because society expects it, that's what the school gives, and
because the school gives it, we (the teachers) have to conform,
and because we have to conform, there's no group work." (T5)

As long as traditional outcomes are valued, it is easy to perpetuate patterns that yield those outcomes:

"It's kind of the old tradition – how we were taught
ourselves at school, you know. It's out there, and the teacher
lectured you and you took notes or whatever and it was pretty
passive . . . and of course we accepted things as they were – I
mean one does as one goes through the system." (T14)

A common fear is that group work is too casual to foster 'real' learning:

"I feel that maybe I'm not getting on with the work,
you know ... A bit relaxed you know or 'laid back' as they
say, and there's not quite the grafting that we should be doing."
(T13)

"Now I would like to do things in a more informal way
- but on the other hand there are pressures from outside ... You
see we are a school competing with another school." (T11)

Given the strength of the academic tradition in schools, it is understandable that group work tends often to be developed first with lower-attaining pupils. This is so in the Atkin School. Some teachers, comfortable with higher-attaining pupils and skilled in more formal patterns of teaching, were remarkably honest in acknowledging the difficulty they have in working with other pupils:

"I can relate a lot better to kids who are like my own
children – do you know what I mean? Sometimes I feel that I
can't get through to the others. I mean, I do the best I can but
I can't sometimes get on their wavelength. They'd be better off
really if they were doing something practical. They'll do anything
rather than sit at a desk." (T13)

It's an easy step from such a view to one which says that group work is essentially a non-academic, because non-teacher-centred, way of learning and therefore more appropriate for the lower-attaining pupils:

"The group work I do is either in the lower years or
with the special educational needs children." (T20)

"I've done it (group work) because it's been necessary
with the very low-ability children ... some of this – it's not
terribly exciting a way out. The point is that they're very
low-ability children who do it. They're enjoying it. They
like doing it. ... This is the best way to keep them
working because after all low ability children – their concentration
is not good. As long as their friend isn't a real idler it's as well
to have them together (in a pair or group) if you can do it."
(T17)

On the whole it seems easier for teachers to work out what group work offers to pupils who are not doing academic work:

"If we get these children to co-operate with each other,
to understand each others' feelings, to appreciate each others'
emotions, how to come to terms with each others' failures
or strengths ... Those who lack confidence tend to grow in
confidence because they know they're not working on their own
as individuals and they are not going to fail as individuals ... I
think it gives them a greater understanding of other people,
of their own problems, how others can compensate for their
weaknesses." (T5)

The teacher here is talking about groups whose
members are all lower attaining children, but other teachers
see group work as more beneficial if the group includes pupils
of different abilities:

"Stronger ones help the weaker ones – working together
is a very useful activity which doesn't find much of a place in
much teaching here." (T2)

"I think it's good (in) that it enables the lesser ability
to be pulled into a higher ability with different ideas – I think
we train kids to be very selfish – they get ideas and they keep
these ideas to themselves." (T19)

But the traffic in ideas is seen as one-way – from the
academically "stronger" pupils to the academically "weaker"
pupils.

Some teachers find an additional professional satisfaction in group work in that they feel they are getting to see
capacities in children that have not been revealed in a class
teaching situation:

"You feel a sense of success when *they* begin to achieve
something – people who would have perhaps achieved very little
before. You can see now that they have got a personal
worth of their own which has probably been ignored by
the school in the past." (T2)

Other positive advantages of group work were mentioned: it helps pupils to develop their own ideas; it allows
them to work more at their own pace; it enables them to
participate on their own terms and encourages the children
to participate – "to be drawn out" – who rarely contribute
in a whole-class activity. Two teachers see group work
as fitting pupils for employment:

"Well I think in school people are encouraged to work

individually far too much. When you leave school whatever you do you're not usually working as an individual. You're either working as a cog in a machine or you're working with other people and sort of for the same ends, not just working for yourself." (T4)

"When you leave school if you're a manager you have to deal with people on the shop floor: if you're on the shop floor you have to be dealt with by a manager, and those kids are going to finish up at one end of the structure or the other." (T18)

Overall – and this is not surprising in a school that has achieved such success in external examinations – teachers tend to see group work as offering experiences that complement rather than contribute to academic learning. But, as we have seen, some teachers, although not perhaps quite ready to take the risk, are certainly considering what benefit group work might bring to more academic courses.

Forming groups

The teachers interviewed have very different attitudes to and strategies for the formation of groups. Some teachers believe that a group will only function well if it is constructed by the teacher or if it includes "a fairly dominant pupil". One teacher acknowledges the influence of his experience as a scoutmaster:

"I would probably have a certain number of group leaders that I knew from experience were capable and able and I would get them thoroughly versed in a certain point that I wanted to make and I would get them then to rehearse that point with a group. Apart from being a teacher I'm a scout leader you see and I see group work working extremely well there every week." (T11)

Others feel that pupils should have responsibility for choosing their working groups and of allocating tasks according to their inside knowledge of what their partners are good at:

"A child who is good at drawing, for example, would be given, not by me but by the group, posters . . . and those that are good at writing are given the job of writing the presentation." (T5)

18

Essentially, teachers who trust pupils more will permit them to manage their own arrangements for working in groups, while those who suspect that in groups, away from the constant surveillance of the teacher, the pupils will "waste their time as children will", tend to take charge of the group formation. The principle of the self-fulfilling prophecy may work here!

A point of disagreement is whether or not the teacher should intervene to make sure that there are girls and boys in each group. Some teachers feel strongly that learning to work across the sexes is more important than free choice of working partners. Having girls in a group, says one teacher (T10), may be a way of tempering the competitive impulse that boys seem, stereotypically, to display. The dilemma, of course, as another teacher points out, is that the pupils themselves may not want to work in mixed-sex groups. One teacher (T13) fears that in mixed-sex groups traditional role models may work to the disadvantage of both boys and girls – the girls are left to do the work and are exploited, and the boys do not learn to participate and collaborate:

"They turn mostly to the girl in the group who does the work and they say 'Right – you organise the thing.' And she's put up as the person who says it (ie makes the presentation). They don't contribute a lot." (T13)

Constraints

As in other schools where we talked with teachers about group work, many explanations were offered as to why the approach is not more widely or consistently used.

Problems of space and time are identified by several teachers as features which prevent them from experimenting with group work or from making it a more regular activity:

"When you're faced with 30 in the class plus very few resources . . . we haven't really got nice areas. You really need a large work base." (T2)

"The rooms that we have by and large don't really lend themselves very well to that kind of thing." (T10)

"It's difficult because the room is small, the tables are large and it's difficult to actually separate the group." (T18)

"We've got 30 odd in the class for a session that's 35 minutes. It's rather difficult to do anything other than the traditional style." (T11)

Shortage of free time in which to develop resources is mentioned by another teacher (T15) as a reason for staying with a more traditional teaching style.

Many teachers reveal anxiety about control and about how others would judge classrooms that are not obviously quiet and orderly:

"You know teachers have this kind of block about noise.
If it's noisy you can't be doing work." (T13)

"Certainly if this was to happen in secondary school
and an outsider went by and there was a lot of noise and
running about, they would think there was no learning going
on." (T11)

"The attitude here is that quiet is control and that noise
is out of control." (T4)

Clearly there is a need to build a new, shared understanding, both within and outside the school, of what conditions learning can flourish in. Here again we see evidence of teachers who are caught at the cross roads – facing the possibilities of a new style of work but fearing that they may be judged according to more conventional criteria.

Teachers also perceive the attitudes and expectations of the pupils themselves as constraining the development of group work:

"Too often they're quite happy to just sit there like little
jugs and let you pour it in ... The number of times one gets a
question from them to say 'Is that right, Sir?' when what they
mean is have I got what you wanted us to get!" (T7)

"It's just a skive as far as they're concerned." (T14)

"Unless you stand over them they won't do it because
that's what they're used to, somebody standing over them."
(T15)

Other teachers see pupils as being too limited by their age and background to make a valuable contribution to group discussion: "They're only little and they're so lacking in experience." A minority of staff hold the view that children are essentially "naughty" and perpetually seeking opportunities to escape from teacherly demands. The fear is that groups, licensed to talk without the teacher being able to monitor all their exchanges, will not address themselves to the task in hand.

The public examination system is seen as placing formidable constraints on the development of group work. For example, the syllabus makes demands that in the view of some teachers can only be met by a traditional teaching style:

"There's such a body of facts to be accumulated and amassed, and the only way that most people think that they can get through in a situation where they've got a whole group of about 30 is the sort of didactic approach." (T2)

"If you did it all by discussion you'd never make it. I'd never get to the end of it because it is just too slow. And if you leave it to them to do the discussing I think it would be even slower." (T8)

"I found it easier to get through the syllabus not using group work . . . I was able to work my way through the syllabus much more quickly making sure that they all got the relevant facts. I found that group work lends itself in my opinion to non-examination work." (T20)

"If there were no examination syllabus I think my own teaching style would be totally radical. I'd turn it round considerably." (T19)

"It's rather difficult to get away from the chalk and talk approach. You see we go out of our way to be fair to them, to say right we'll give the maximum chance to be in the top set. And as soon as you've got large numbers in that group, just from the point of view of order within the room, you've just got to be on top of them." (T11)

Teachers are understandably unwilling to venture on to the ground of new pedagogy unless they are convinced that the level of achievement can be preserved: "I'm dubious as to whether it's better than class teaching." (T12) There are several unknowns, the main one being whether pupils would learn the same things as effectively through group work. As one teacher (T20) says, her pupils clearly enjoy their work much more when they can participate in group activity – but will they be as well-prepared for the public examination, she asks – or might they "get better results"? This teacher voices the anxiety that many colleagues seem to be feeling but a colleague offers evidence that is reassuring:

"Whenever I've done anything that you would call group

work I've found on the whole that the standard has been a lot better than if it's been done singly." (T17)

Certainly the advent of GCSE will give teachers a legitimate reason for taking more risks with group work:

"GCSE – that will require more change, more discussion work and more group work." (T18)

"With the new GCSE there's an awful lot of emphasis being placed on investigations." (T9).

But there's also some cynicism:

"When GCSE comes I think people will be teaching it exactly the same as they've taught O-level and CSE because no money has been put into in-service training, or very little."(T2)

It seems that initial training has not generally provided the kind of opportunity which would help teachers to feel confident about what group work is, what place it might have in their subject, and whether it is worth developing as part of their repertoire of teaching strategies. As one teacher said:

"I think the majority of teachers in our sort of school were trained in the sixties and you didn't have any in-service training to make you see things in a totally new perspective." (T2)

And insecurity can easily breed rejection:

"I don't know how to go about group work." (T12)

"I'm not personally in favour of group work. I haven't done a lot." (T5)

"I think because we're not very familar with it we may totally disagree with it." (T9)

The way forward

Opportunities for in-service training in the immediate area are not great. As one teacher said:

"I think a lot of staff feel very isolated. At one time this area used to have panels of like-minded teachers meeting together ... All that has gone by the board so teachers don't really get an opportunity to meet with other staff from other schools." (T2)

There is clearly a need for external support to help interested teachers explore new approaches with confidence, but, as the interviews reveal in a striking way, there is a large amount of rich individual experience in the school that is not being shared – sometimes even with colleagues in the same department. One teacher, for instance, has undertaken an intensive study of her own attempts to introduce discussion-based work. She recorded pupil talk in small groups, analysed it to see where pupils were able to help each other with problems and where they still had to seek help from the teacher, and what amount of talk was 'on-task' as opposed to 'off-task'. (T21)

The school's recently appointed Director of Studies is eager to help create a forum for discussing teaching and learning: "We want to analyse what is good practice in the school and translate it across to other areas." (T3) Interestingly schools seem to need an event, a new person, a new technology, or an outside pressure to create an opportunity for change which they can all respond to. Certainly at the Atkin school the tide seems right for launching a scheme which will allow teachers to share experience and develop new teaching strategies. Individually, teachers are raising very important questions about group work and learning. For example:

● do pupils actually spend a lot of time when in groups talking about non-work topics?

● how does a teacher judge what is irrelevant to the pursuit of a task?

● is chat the product of an insufficiently engaging task, and therefore the teacher's responsibility – or does it represent a "natural tendency" in pupils to avoid work?

● does chat sometimes provide a necessary period of intellectual rest time which is in fact conducive to learning? What might be its positive functions?

● do teachers dismiss some pupil talk as "irrelevant chat" when in fact they are merely failing to understand the logic of the pupils' world?

● is it desirable, and if so, feasible, to assess the individual's contribution to a task which group members have tackled collaboratively?

These are just a few of the questions that individual teachers are asking themselves and that could be identified and developed through group discussion among the staff as a whole.

A shift towards more group work would not of course be just a matter of adding something to the teacher's repertoire of teaching strategies. Taken seriously, it could imply some fundamental rethinking of values. As one teacher suggested:

"I think you have to learn to value the opinions of the students and allow them to take responsibility for what they're doing." (T2)

In a school with a residual academic perspective on learning, and where the lower achieving pupils are taught in special groups, such a change would not be easy for all teachers, but with time created to allow groups of like-minded colleagues to work together on developing and evaluating new approaches change could be accomplished.

Perhaps the major challenge to the school's development of new teaching and learning strategies is the tension between the personal/social and intellectual development of their pupils. On the whole, different teaching strategies are used for different groups of pupils and this approach reflects a fundamental cleavage in the school: chalk and talk is for the academic pupils and group work is for the less-academic pupils.

On the other hand there are many signs that individual teachers, sensing that the school is at the crossroads of change, are keen to support the Head in thinking through what a comprehensive school is and to participate in some concerted and supportive programme that will help them to develop different ways of working. The experience already exists in the school, but it is scattered and as yet largely unanalysed and unshared.

THE BRIGHTWOOD SCHOOL: ROOM AT THE TOP?

Background

The setting is a popular East coast sea-side resort with a population of 40,000. The Brightwood school came into existence in 1973 through the amalgamation of a girls' grammar school and a secondary school. There are around 1,600 pupils in the school with a sixth form of 150. The upper school (Forms 3-6) is in a modern building on the edge of the town; the lower school (first and second forms) is housed a mile away in the old building of the Girls' Grammar School. The school is 10 form entry 11-18 and has eight feeder primary schools which serve it and the other comprehensive school nearby.

In the first year, pupils are taught in mixed-ability classes. In the second year they are set for maths, French, English and science. There is provision for setting in all subjects in the third year. At the time of the study fourth and fifth year pupils were divided into bands; however, since the advent of GCSE, the same choice of subjects is available to all fourth and fifth year pupils, though within subjects there continues to be setting. The school is pleased with its success in examination passes. There is a flourishing sixth form where the A-level pass rate is around 80 per cent. Destinations of fifth formers last year in percentage terms were as follows:

Stayed on in 6th form	:	22
Went to FE College	:	12
Entered employment	:	17
YTS	:	42
No information	:	7

A fair proportion of pupils go on to university, polytechnic and the local College of Technology; three went to Oxford in the previous year.

Unemployment in the region is high (around 14%) though the Head predicts some change in this trend:

"The future of this area is looking up. We've got a motorway coming through, and the airport has been developed — more gas has been found in the North Sea and so on. That's fine

25

but I think that they are looking for high technology experts so the future is pretty grim for the weak academic child." (M4)

How do the teachers perceive group work?

Some teachers see benefits for *all* pupils in group work since it may develop sensitivity to others, communication skills, and the growth of understanding and powers of criticism.

"In my subject group work is vital. It's part of the socialisation process, learning to get on with one another . . . It's all understanding of people, of people in society. Whereas if you're doing maths you're doing maths, but we have a very wide field." (T9) (Drama teacher)

An English teacher makes his analysis of the difference between formal teaching and group work:

"With formal teaching there's a learning process you know, the pupils are given the material, they have to learn it. Quite separately from everyone else, unlike life. And that is an artificial process in my view. Using group work they're learning from each other very often informally, the odd comment here, this idea of co-operating with someone else to solve a common problem. Much of the knowledge they gain is internalised without them actually thinking they've learned anything. I think that's basically the difference between group work and other methods." (T2)

And he would argue that this learning is more likely to be retained even though he is aware that many pupils do not consider the process as 'real work'. In fact he views group work as the most natural way of learning:

"I think very often when you're using group work you see the pupil as you've never seen the pupil before. That's suddenly a human being there; he's operating in a normal way." (T2)

This is also demonstrated in one lesson where the study of Athenian democracy was related to contemporary issues:

"I did a lesson with a low ability class about how the Athenians ostracised people and I said to them, 'Is there anybody you would like to ostracise?' (It was at the time of the miners' strike.) I said, 'You might want to ostracise me for various reasons. I wouldn't mind but you have got to give a reasoned appeal to the Assembly to ostracise whoever you

26

choose' . . . They were quite happy and most of it was Margaret Thatcher and Arthur Scargill. But as we were going round, there was one little boy who was very distressed and he said 'I don't want to do mine', and he pushed his paper to me and said, 'I chose her'. It was a teacher. So I said, 'What's made you change your mind?' and he said, 'As I've been listening I wanted to get rid of her for the wrong reasons. It only affects *me. I'm* lazy in her lesson and I can see it's got to be for the good of the people.' I felt that for a low ability child to pick that up – I was delighted." (M3)

Another aspect of group work is explained by the Music teacher who asks pupils to work in groups to discuss one another's work:

"We offer criticism. If we were doing a project about outer space then the other groups would be able to say whether they felt musically speaking it gave the right feeling and whether or not if they wrote a sort of science fiction story about something happening in outer space they got the right atmosphere about it, the right tone colour for musical instruments, the right sounds. And that is something that children have to learn to live with – that criticism is part of adult life. The biggest difficulty is monitoring it so that it's not destructive." (T11)

An English teacher uses problem solving group work to develop pupils' understanding of how a narrative is constructed:

"The most motivating thing in learning I find is in having a problem to solve. So if I wanted to teach fractured narrative (the idea that we bridge gaps in narratives) then the best way of doing this is by giving the pupils the problem to solve for themselves. In that way, through co-operative group work, they gain insights which I can't give them." (T4)

Here is an example of his approach. The children's task is to solve a mystery drawn from detective fiction using six extracts each describing a mysterious occurrence. It is up to the pupils to decide whether to link the extracts or treat them separately. The lesson is very lively and after a period of small group discussion, a larger group forms in the centre of the classroom. They have pooled the six extracts and are discussing how they can co-operatively form these into one whole story. The students are challenged by the task and experience directly the value of sharing and exploring solutions together. They are developing language skills as they debate and analyse the mystery. In addition, they are learning about the structure of stories and about the control which an author can have over the writing process. This group activity can then feed back into individual composing and enhance the growth of the concept of story.

A Classics teacher finds that translation seems to lend itself well to collaborative effort:

"You will often find in Latin that there are perhaps five or six ways in which a word can be translated according to its context. For example, the Latin word 'audacia', which is the foot of our word 'audacious', can be translated as 'boldness', 'recklessness' or 'daring'. You've got a smaller amount of basic vocabulary but each word can be given its own particular nuance in its own context."

The pupils respond to the challenge:

"You get people saying, 'Well, boldness is a basic meaning for that word!' Another might say, 'Well, recklessness fits in here better in this context.' But that's where these subtle variations in translation come into their own."

Fortunately, he adds, the GCSE examination places more emphasis on the natural English style of translation than the strictly literal one which gained high marks in the past. Furthermore, by working collaboratively and sharing findings, pupils are able to cover far more ground than one individual could:

"Take the example of a topic that is in the GCSE syllabus – Pompeii. The information can only be obtained from reading through the relevant sections of 10 or 11 different books. If a group works on that they can minimise the mechanical difficulties of getting through a topic, make an accurate account of that information, weed out things which are useful to the group as a whole, and present their findings to the whole class."

This kind of project-based work seems to lend itself to group work and gives the students experience of a range of perspectives on a topic. The responsibility shifts to the pupils:

"Previously I would have looked through that myself and produced a worksheet for them but it is interesting to give them more responsibility in planning their own course of study."

The interviews reveal many examples where imaginative group work like this takes place. But in general such positive evaluations of group work methods are rare. The majority of teachers seem to feel more secure with a formal, traditional teaching style.

We interviewed 18 teachers from a range of departments in the school and without exception they describe the predominant teaching style in the school as traditional. The Head confirms this although he acknowledges the value of group work and predicts that its use as a method will increase in the next few years, largely because of its inclusion in the new GCSE syllabuses. He thinks that one major benefit of group work for young people will be a greater fluency in language and communication skills; a second will be the social and intellectual benefits arising from the experience of working together on field work and other projects.

However, while he recognises the need to move away from the predominantly traditional teaching style in the school he admits that the development of group work is not such a high priority as "the many other issues which need urgent attention", specifically "profiling, self-assessment, active tutorial work, counselling skills and in-service training in connection with GCSE." He feels that group work is something for which teachers rather than the Head could take responsibility: "in the end it depends on the individual teacher with the individual class and how they feel on the day and the enthusiasm they've got." (M4)

One Deputy Head, an English teacher, highlights the dilemmas faced by any teacher in the school who attempted to introduce innovative teaching methods such as group work:

"Our own thinking is that unless we try to nurture
group work as part of a methodology of a particular approach to
learning, it gets edged out by traditional commitments, such as
exam pressure, time of teachers." (M1)

There is strong evidence from the interviews that most teachers in the school believe that a formal teaching style is the most appropriate for academic work. According to a maths teacher, group work does not necessarily benefit all pupils who take part in it:

"There are not a lot of young people who can actually
work as a group where there is a meeting of minds. It requires a
fair amount of intellect and the problem with working in groups
in school, for instance in maths, is that if you let kids design
their own groups, it tends to be the dominant person and you end
up with people in groups whose contribution is minimal, and I
can't see that it is a learning process for them." (T14)

An English teacher questions the academic value of
group work:

"I'm suspicious of it simply because it does seem to provide
opportunities for some people to become passengers and to
create a situation where it's impossible to gauge the amount of
contribution which individual people make." (T17)

One teacher identifies two contrasting styles of
teaching history in the school, one highly structured,
formal and teacher-centred, the other discursive, informal
and pupil-centred. In each case the teaching is thought
to be excellent and the syllabus is covered, but strong
anxieties are, it seems, expressed by sixth formers about the
discussion-based approach:

"Some of the 6th-formers come to us and say, 'Well, I
prefer this style because at least you end up with handouts and
you've got them and you've got something to learn. But you
know with the other we have a double lesson and we just end
up arguing all the time." (M2)

A maths teacher indicates how threatening traditional
teachers find the physical lay-out of classrooms where
co-operative group work takes place:

"It's a problem for people who teach in a traditional
manner. Then they have pupils with their backs to them."
(T10)

Another makes a very clear distinction between his
behaviour in academic and vocational classes:

"My own code of conduct is more rigid with the academic
course. ... I've been wary of using group work with
the more academic. I've felt constrained by getting through the
syllabus ... An outsider coming in to compare the two lessons
would see a stark contrast in acceptable behaviour." (T15)

Of his CPVE students he says:

"With the vocational course, being part of a team, they

realise they are part of a group. They see me with a different hat on as head of year, but once in the classroom when we're together they can take the lesson over and I become a member of the class." (T15)

A science teacher makes a similar comparison between examination classes and vocational courses such as science/industry:

"It's a different attitude entirely to the actual teaching. These are children at the lower end of the academic scale. The curriculum is aimed at far more practical skills." (T13)

And a CPVE teacher says of her work:

"I basically deal with lower ability. A very different view you'll have from me as compared to someone who's teaching at the top." (T8)

She adds that whereas maths teachers "have knowledge to impart and it's very much chalk-and-talk," for her vocational pupils it is different:

"It's essential that work is done in groups. We're very much aware that we're trying to develop them as people ... With CPVE, it's an ideal vehicle really to encourage people to co-operate and discuss and realise other people's opinions." (T8)

Group work in the context of industry

There has been concern in the school that sixth formers who are studying for two A levels are not using their free time as constructively as they might. As a result, a group of teachers have liaised with managers from industry to find ways in which they could teach theory and link it with reality by involving the students in company-based work.

One outcome of the partnership between the school and a local company has been the development of the GCSE *British Industrial Society*. Since 30 per cent of the marks are awarded for project work, the collaboration with industry offers an ideal opportunity for giving students experience of solving real problems and of learning to work productively as a group. The company is keen for the course to be taught largely on a group basis in order to parallel management strategies in industry, and has arranged for the teacher to

31

gain experience of being a participant in a management training course on team work. This involves the learning of strategies for problem-solving by working constructively and productively in a team. The teacher gave very favourable reports of the course.

"We learned how to find the strength of individuals within our teams and use these strengths, these abilities, these skills in order to achieve a particular goal that we were set. We were taught about the value of active listening, supportive comments; we learned about organizational ability within the group and the need to review what the group experience has given us."

Ideally, she adds, that was how the firm would have liked to see the course run in school. However, there have been a number of difficulties in actually putting these ideas into practice in the school setting. There is the very practical problem of the use of time. Here is one example:

"On the management course we were given a task and 40 minutes to prepare a plan for approaching this task. For the first 30 minutes we were getting absolutely nowhere. We were trying to feed in ideas but what we really needed to do was all shut up for a few minutes and think quietly. Then suddenly the ideas started to come and we could order them." (M2)

This teacher doubts that pupils would see the value of spending time in reflection and feels that such an activity would be seen as unproductive. Furthermore, in a single lesson, there would not normally be time for the incubation period to be seen to be fruitful. Tolerance of the whole range of behaviour involved in the generation of ideas (from the silence as each individual formulates thoughts to the noise of brainstorming) could involve a radical change in both teachers' and pupils' conceptions of productive work, but group work, she feels herself, is not compatible with study for an examination course:

"That's where the clash occurs. If I'm doing an examination course, I feel obliged for the students' sake to have covered so much material in a certain amount of time, and group work is very time-consuming."

Yet one can also sense her disappointment that the course lacked the respectability of more traditional subjects despite its obvious relevance to industrial society.

It is clear that productive links can be made in work that requires partnership between schools and industry but both teachers and pupils need to be clear about what the benefits are. In this school, academic students are not at all sure that group work meets their needs: "If they are honestly academics then bits of paper are important to them."

It is in fact safer to experiment with group work methods when pupils are less able:

"If you think you've got weak students then you tend
to play down the paper qualifications and go for doing work for
its own sake and how industry might view it." (M2)

Two courses which rely heavily on the co-operative group work approach are the Science/Industry Course and the Certificate in Pre-Vocational Education (CPVE), both designed for the needs of the less-academic pupil. The Science/Industry course has a vocational aim. There is a syllabus to follow, course work assessment and an examination, but the content of the course is very flexible. Since the course is designed to prepare young people for the world of industry, it has a work experience component in the fifth year consisting of one full day per week and two one-week blocks. Pupils stay with the same employer throughout their work experience. Firms are carefully selected in order to give the young people a sense of continuity and the opportunity to develop a feeling of identification with colleagues at work. There is also the advantage that the employer gets to know the trainee well enough to write a reference for future job applications. For the most part, the teacher in charge of this course tries to arrange placements with small firms where (in his words) the young person is more likely "to feel part of a group."

What are the benefits of this kind of course for the pupil? In the words of one teacher, the experience of collaborating with others generates ideas "at a level that is beyond them individually." The young people learn to work with others who are not necessarily their close friends and, on occasion, with individuals whom they do not like. The teacher also stresses the value of the sense of group identity which builds up in that it helps the young people to acquire "the discipline of work":

"The smaller the group, the better that works. In a large
group the lazier people can hide within the mass;
within the small group they just haven't got the chance
to, so it does encourage the lazier end to put in a bit more
work." (T13)

In CPVE, one example of successful group work has
been the formation of a committee whose task was to organise
activities such as a children's picnic or an old people's lunch.
The teachers have found that this kind of practical exercise
is more involving for the pupils than, say, discussion about
controversial issues. Furthermore, the fact that the pupils have
their own base in the sixth form block helps to foster a sense
of group identity, and, as a result, they become "more aware
of each other and more aware of other people's needs, and to
some extent become less selfish in their views, because they're
having to adhere to other people's wishes which is something
some of them have never really been aware of before." (T8)
Contrary to expectation, there are few discipline problems in
CPVE clases:

"Once you relax that little bit and let them negotiate,
the discipline problems lessen considerably." (T8)

Conclusion

Group work seems to flourish in vocational courses for
the less academic pupil. It is in these subjects that teachers
refer most to qualities which collaboration can facilitate, such
as "sensitivity to others", "a sense of responsibility", "maturity", "communication skills" and "a preparation for the world
of work." By contrast, in traditional academic subjects teachers
are more likely to express doubts about the effectiveness of
group work as a learning strategy. It was more common in
the course of the interviews to hear that group work is not
appropriate because "you need a body of knowledge before you
can discuss," or because "individualised learning strategies are
more appropriate in my subject area," (maths) "assessment of
group work is a problem," (English) "creativity is an individual
process," (Art) and "it's the amount of content that stops
us." (science) Pressure to follow a syllabus and to prepare
pupils for examinations seem to be experienced as powerful
constraints on the development of group work in academic

subjects. Pupils too express reservations about group work in the context of preparing for examinations.

At the same time, as we have seen, there are many individual examples of group work, including role play, simulation exercises, discussions, exercises to deepen critical awareness, problem-solving groups, business games. These activities depend on the initiative of individual teachers rather than formal school policy. Indeed, as we saw earlier, the Head has stated that group work is best left to individual initiative. One side effect of this is that understanding of group work methods does not appear to be widely shared amongst colleagues and this can lead to misperceptions about where group work is actually happening. "People don't realise what other staff are doing, which I think is a very sad shame," said one teacher. Another teacher suggests that lack of communication occurs because staff are reluctant to open up their work to each other for fear of being judged. Knowledge of colleagues' collaborative methods seems to be gained only indirectly, for example by the disarrangement of chairs in a classroom.

Teachers who *are* developing co-operative learning strategies with pupils still feel that they are working in a predominantly traditional context which is slow to change. A number of teachers say that they would do more group work if only they had experienced some training. "If we'd been brought up on group teaching we'd be doing it now."

One teacher, challenging the idea that you could leave the development of group work to individual initiative, suggests that there are too many pitfalls, especially in the early stages. But where teachers have had first-hand experience in group work, for example in counselling courses or management training courses run by industry, they are more willing to experiment with group work – and soon see that the results can be very rewarding:

"I think children are fantastic at being able to cope with
all different levels and I think once they've tried it they enjoy
it." (M3)

In the year since we interviewed teachers in Brightwood School, considerable changes have taken place. A major impact on the use of group work across the curriculum has come from the requirements of the GCSE syllabus. The growing experience of the teachers in a whole range of group work strategies, coupled with the focus on collaborative learning in the GCSE syllabus, is resulting in a new emphasis in the school on this kind of approach. Already in a number of departments it is a policy that there should be more co-ordination of group work methods and increased opportunities for individual staff members to share ideas on the development of co-operative learning strategies for all pupils whether in academic or vocational courses.

"With formal teaching there's a learning process – the pupils are given the material, they have to learn it, quite separately from anything else, unlike life. And this is an artificial process in my view. Using group work they're learning from each other, often informally – the odd comment here, co-operation to solve a problem. It's internalised without them actually thinking they've learned anything ... But the system says 'If it's worthwhile you write it down, but if it isn't you can talk about it.' That may change." (English teacher)

THE CLAYTON SCHOOL: "BEGINNING TO GROW!"

Background

This study is based on transcripts of interviews carried out with 20 teachers at the Clayton school, each of which lasted around 30/35 minutes. There was also a longer interview with the Head teacher. The teachers who took part in the interviews were selected by the Head in order to represent a spectrum of attitudes towards group work in the school. Thus some were opposed to it, some very committted to it and some did not hold strong views on the subject. All expressed their views freely and no one refused to be interviewed.

Interviews were held with: the Head teacher; a Deputy Head; Head of Home Economics; Head of English; Acting Head of Economics; Head of History; teacher in charge of PE; two English teachers; two social and personal education teachers (one in charge); two craft and design teachers; two Maths teachers; a Music teacher; two science teachers; a languages teacher; a special needs teacher; a geography teacher.

The school, a comprehensive of around 1,100 pupils, is set in a pleasant environment on the edge of a large northern city. The school has five main feeder Middle Schools of which three draw their pupils from a mixture of private and council housing and two from mainly council estates. There are very few pupils from ethnic minority families; the majority are from white working-class homes. The area is a stable one in that many of the parents themselves attended local schools. The atmosphere in the school is welcoming and friendly. Most students appear to enjoy school and there is good will and support on the part of the parents.

Last year fifth form destinations were, in percentage terms, as follows:

6th form	13.3
FE college	10.5
YTS	45
Job	9.5
Not known/unemployed	21.7

Recent curriculum change in the school

In 1983 three curriculum initiatives were introduced. The first was an inter-disciplinary, non-examination course for all pupils in social and personal education. The second was a programme of enrichment named 'activities' in which blocks of time were set aside for all pupils in years two-five to experience a range of negotiable activities (eg working with senior citizens, making music, playing games) which would enhance the students' development outside the traditional academic curriculum. The third initiative offered pupils a wider range of non-examination options in areas such as rural studies, design for living, home maintenance.

At the beginning of the present study this was how the curriculum was organized. In the Lower school all pupils studied English, maths, science, languages, history, geography, design studies, home economics, social and personal education (SPE), PE, music and (in the third year) economics. Two periods in the week were set aside for the Activities programme. In the Upper School, all pupils studied English, maths, SPE and PE (37 per cent of the timetable). There were five option blocks and two activities programmes (63 percent of the timetable). These subjects were reviewed regularly and their relevance to pupils' needs was an issue of concern.

Some members of staff are happy with the way in which innovations have been integrated into the existing structure, but others question the structure itself and are searching for ways in which a more fundamental change might be made. In the words of one Deputy Head:
"The fate of the two most radical areas of innovation –
SPE and 'activities' – is instructive. SPE aspired to be a whole educational project, a coherent inter-disciplinary initiative.
Over four years, it has become a subject department not much unlike any other. This is not the fault of those who worked to set it up and have taught it with a great deal of commitment and imagination. Rather, it was inevitable in a
school where group approaches and cross-curricular practice have remained undeveloped. 'Activities' has become progressively more at risk because of staffing reduction and is ... becoming disoriented by a loss of purpose. The essential difficulty with both is that they are trying to compensate for the inertia of the rest of the curriculum."

His point is that the departmental structure and the curriculum (with the exception of SPE and activities) would not have been out of place in a traditional grammar school.

The Head highlights the difficulties involved in any attempt to introduce change into an established system:

"Throughout education, and even within institutions perceived to be 'vanguard' in curriculum terms, lines of development are dogged by an entrenched conservatism. Within particular schools, this conservatism is consistently reinforced from a variety of sources – personal, inter-personal and structural.

The events in this school over the last few years would bear this out. Whilst the initiatives of the early 1980's clearly demonstrated some commitment to change, it is doubtful whether the real issues were ever addressed. In consequence, the curriculum was developed by accretion and addition, and the sum total of the experience presented to pupils in the classroom and beyond remained essentially as before. More of the same, if more attractively packaged!"

He goes on:

"Whilst timetable structures may well have changed, the attitudes and values which underpin those structures . . . *haven't*. You can dress up the structure of the formal curiculum to look what you will. Once in the classroom, however, unless the values and attitudes which the teacher *presents* to the task are . . . radically different from that which is the grammarian tradition, then invariably, for the pupils, nothing changes.

The assumption is made that if we shift the structures, then children will *per se* get a different experience, and this doesn't follow. Shifting structures does not inevitably shift people's hearts and minds, or the methodologies and approaches which they adopt in the classroom.

What you're asking teachers to do is to move away from the position in which they enjoy unlimited power and responsibility for learning to the learners themselves . . . And that's asking a lot of people who even now are coming through the tertiary system, through universities and colleges, still believing that education is about standing at the front and dispensing wisdom."

He argues too that there are few role-models – at

school, in FE and in higher education – to demonstrate that there is a wider range of teaching methods than the traditional didactic ones:

"The focus in HE, in FE, is still subject based. The focus is on content, on knowledge, and information and data. There is precious little emphasis on skills, on concepts. Young people come to us in their first year of teaching and survive by promoting dissemination of content. Their experience of schools and, crucially, their training prepares them for little else. They therefore find it hard to become facilitators of other people's learning and to adopt all the methodologies that go along with that."

Against this background, further innovations were in progress at the time of this study. Two are seen as particularly relevant to the theme of co-operative group work. The first concerned the school's participation in a city-wide initiative, School Focused Secondment (SFS), in which a team of five teachers worked together for a year on a coherent set of curricular tasks, one aspect of which was an investigation of group work as an effective learning method. The other innovation was a project designed to change attitudes towards mental handicap. Inter-disciplinary teams of teachers collaborated with teachers from schools for the mentally handicapped, parents, social workers, community workers and others to design a module lasting one week which would give students at the school the opportunity to work alongside children with a range of mental and physical disabilities, to share experiences and learn about one another. These two initiatives are explored in some detail in this case study. But first we look at responses by the 20 teachers and the Head to the open-ended interviews which were carried out at the beginning of the study. These give valuable insights into the context within which change is taking place in the school.

Perceptions of group work

During the interviews, it became clear that attitudes towards group work as an effective learning method covered a wide spectrum. Some teachers are clearly enthusiastic:

"In a group situation kids make collaborative leaps and

bounds. The process is a shared one of moving on from what one individual has contributed."

"Almost everything is better done through group work engagement than through giving children facts."

"I would argue that group work is necessary for kids' cognitive development as well as their social development."

"Group work is more productive."

"Pupils can learn things from each other."

"Pupils develop a sense of responsibility when they work in groups."

"I think the old way isn't civilised."

"Personal relationships are important in learning. The experience of using group work in SPE has brought this home to me."

Others express reservations about the value of group work:

"It's naive and idealistic. It could not work."

"I have grave doubts about group work. Groups of more than two do a lot of chat and not a lot of work."

"If I have to choose, work with the individual wins every time."

"They become little clubs. You don't get the work done."

"Group work is clearly appropriate in social and personal education (SPE) but not suitable for exam courses."

To teachers who are committed to the idea of working collaboratively group work is seen as a highly effective way of utilising the resources and abilities of students:

"We do a lot of group work because we cover more in that way and I think the class gets more out of it. You have more going on and it has that cumulative effect at the end when you can draw together all the strands that they have been working on." (T4)

"Even the ones who are tempted off the track get more done in the five minutes that they are on track than they would listening solidly to me for a whole lesson."

Value is placed on the capacity of pupils to take responsibility for their own learning:

"I'm a great believer in giving them the germ of an idea and letting them get on with it."

41

These teachers also emphasise the fact that through group work pupils are more likely to find a voice for their ideas and to develop the capacity for taking the perspective of others. One points out that "group work creates a warm environment in which young people work effectively together *and* develop good relationships" and applauded the emphasis (eg in the GCSE syllabus) on communication skills, listening, self-expression, empathy and co-operation. Despite this awareness of the value of group work, however, some teachers indicate their frustration at not being able to develop their ideas to the full.

Here are some examples. A science teacher draws parallels with the world of work and stresses the benefits to be gained from group work. He points out its value in improving the self-confidence of girls, and thereby giving them a stronger belief in their own capacity to think scientifically. (T18) However, he declares that, although he would like to develop children's problem-solving abilities through group work, he feels constrained by the syllabus, especially in the Upper School, and by the need to identify individual performances within the group rather than its collaborative effort.

One English teacher, while recognising the difficulties facing teachers who introduced group work methods in traditional subject teaching, is personally convinced that group work facilitates both social and intellectual development and that "in terms of maximising kids' individual contributions, group work has to be the most effective". Since most of his lessons involve some form of 'group work engagement', pupils have come to expect it as part of normal classroom activity. Yet he still finds that many pupils and staff are still unclear about the benefits which could grow out of this method of working. Ironically, although young people find group work demanding and challenging, some still doubt that it is 'real work':

"The classic utterance I've had is when kids used to ask me
'Is this real English?' That was their reaction to oral work of
any kind . . . Their view of English was probably answering
questions out of a book. However, my impression is that students
now more readily accept group work."

Despite his commitment to group work as an effective learning method, he recognises that on occasions staff might use it less in the fourth and fifth year "because of pressure to get through assignments". And an SPE teacher points out:

"I wonder if it's the case where the accent is not on exams
that it's easier to get into groups because the pupils feel there's
nothing to be lost." (T3)

Teachers who are not happy about group work offer a number of reasons. Some point out the stressfulness of handing over responsibility for their own learning to the pupils:

"They've got to learn how to think and talk, and they haven't
done it much."

Others equate group work with "lack of structure" and so are very reluctant to use it. For example, one teacher considers that the personal encounters involved in the process of group work are threatening and "could distract students from the task of learning." Others experience a more general concern about the management of groups in terms both of discipline and equality of contribution:

"You're working with one group and the other group's doing
goodness knows what on the other side of the room."

"A couple dominate and then the quieter ones haven't said
anything in the entire discussion."

Some anxiety about group work is linked to subject specialism and the mastery of skills:

"I value co-operation as a preparation for *life*, but I do not
find that it relates specifically to maths."

"In my subject (History) they haven't got the expertise
to discuss it."

"Craft is individualised if you are in an examination group."

Several teachers from different subjects indicate that they might do more group work if only the conditions made it possible:

"If I had more time a lot of good work could come from
group work."

Emerging themes
One strong theme seems to emerge from these perspectives. There is a tension between some individuals' wish to

develop a wider variety of teaching strategies, including group work, on the one hand and an equally strong pull back to traditional modes of instruction. The tradition of didactic teaching is in most settings very slow to change:

"With my grammar school background and as a grammar school teacher I tend towards the traditional." (T13)

"It's not enough to co-operate. You need to give them some knowledge and content." (T19)

"They just can't be presented with this mass of evidence and say 'Right sort it out.' This is where the didactic approach comes in. You've got to explain, you've got to draw their attention to this and that, you see. I suppose it's a skill in itself, of paying attention to you for some time in the lesson, and actually looking at the evidence . . ." (T17)

For newly qualified teachers, it is a very intimidating system to challenge:

"You are put into a system, like when you start at this school when there is no group work or very little group work and everything is prepared for you. It is very easy to follow the same lines . . . When I do use group work it reminds me of how useful it is. Then you slip back into your old ways of doing things." (T9)

There is also a strong feeling that in the hands of an inexperienced teacher there are great risks involved in the use of group work:

"It wouldn't necessarily be that group work is always good and traditional methods bad. For a weak and vulnerable teacher, group work can actually be a recipe for chaos, because the relationship has got to grow through confidence. Allowing the kids to discuss things, to work together, to co-operate, depends on the chemistry of the group. At its worst it can throw up all the hostilities and the potential problems." (T12)

The examination system of course reinforces the power of traditional methods, and the constraints of following a set syllabus is mentioned by many teachers as a reason for relying on whole-class instruction:

"I think most people's teaching focuses on content because of syllabuses. Teachers teach the middle of the whole class and use a didactic style of teaching rather than setting up separate work for different groups within that class." (T14)

But there is also some evidence – understandable in the present national climate of frenzied change – of a resistance to further change and a longing to consolidate existing skills:

"We've had our hands full over the last six or seven years
with all sorts of developments and so I'm afraid that group work
has been one of the ones that I personally and I think the rest of
the department put fairly low in the order of priorities. And it will
probably remain fairly low down in the order of priorities."

A second major theme concerns the organisation of group work itself:

"Group work is often very threatening to teachers because
your lesson can appear to be out of control, not just to the person
who goes past your door but to yourself, because clearly you're giving
away a certain amount of power to the kids, and if you're not used
to working that way it can be very unsettling." (M1)

Even teachers who are generally confident in their management of groups mention the stress involved:

"After a good lesson you feel it's been very exciting. Good
things have happened and kids have got involved in it, but when you
get the opposite happening it's far more depressing . . . It's always
going to be a much more challenging way of working than traditional
teaching." (T.11)

"Group work requires a lot more careful organisation than
a teacher-taught lesson . . . Unless that structure's in place, unless
you give the pupils the possibility of coherence and development, it
won't happen." (M1)

A number of those who are committed to group work expressed frustration at the lack of opportunity to work collaboratively with colleagues, especially if they wanted to change traditional ways of working:

"You cannot do it on your own. Just one person cannot
start changing the syllabus. You hit a brick wall before you
even start." (T9)

There are too few opportunities for staff to learn from one another because staff are so busy and have little 'free' time for sharing:

"What I need is the experience of other people's experience."
(T13)

"There's not as much chance to work with other people as there

45

should be. I would like to see a lot more opportunity to be observed because you get feedback and to observe colleagues. It would be good to see head of departments operating – even in a completely different subject area." (T11)

"I would like to bring it up as a topic in a departmental meeting and find out what other people do. But really, because I don't have pupils working in groups, I'm not confident myself." (T5)

"I believe that the way that kids learn and the processes that are involved is equal to the way that teachers learn, whether it be in-service work or staff development in school. These processes are the same. They have to be actively involved, have ownership of ideas, have evaluation built in; there's got to be negotiation and consultation."

The facilitation of change

What direction is the school going in now? To the Head the process of change in the school continues. He focuses first on the interplay between people and the structures within which they operate:

"Actually shifting the way in which people operate, perceive their role within a learning environment is the difficult bit to achieve . . ."

At the same time:

"Structures are important too because they underpin particular ways of thinking and doing things and they are supportive to particular ways of thinking and doing. It's fundamentally a question of harnessing commitment and harnessing energy sympathetically and with purpose and with direction."

Without that commitment, structural change will not work:

"It's not just about structures. It's about hearts and minds. Actually shifting attitudes is that much more difficult because it is that much more inner self. Such is the task which confronts us."

How is this being achieved? One solution is to create opportunities for staff to have more direct experience of working collaboratively themselves. This is particularly true of young teachers new to the profession who may, in their struggle to survive, sacrifice experiential ways of working in the classroom.

Without the support of more experienced staff, there is the danger that they fall back on the safety of didactic teaching methods. The Head comments:

"It's a very lengthy task, and it requires that we have people around within schools who have a different view of what schools are about. We have to have a shift out of context in which we consider ourselves to be teachers and into a context where we consider ourselves to be facilitators of learning."

The School Focused Secondment (SFS) is an example of one important attempt to bring teachers together from different schools and different subject areas within the same school to examine the curriculum and explore ways in which learning may best be facilitated. Each secondary school seconded up to five teachers full-time during the year 1986-7 to work on curriculum development. The SFS team from Clayton School summarised key issues which teachers from the school had identified at a staff meeting early in the year. (For the purposes of this case-study we will look at aspects which are most relevant to co-operative group work rather than present an exhaustive report of the whole SFS programme.) Teachers had suggested that the SFS team should consider:

- children's learning processes;
- the need for 'child-centred' learning strategies;
- 'active learning' methods including group work as demonstrated by good practice in the school;
- the most effective use of resources to facilitate learning.

Staff had also expressed concern about ways in which 'compartmentalisation of the curriculum' could prevent pupils from making connections and from integrating knowledge, skills and experience. Teachers, it was felt, could play a more active part in creating the kind of environment in which children could be made aware of different perspectives on an issue, could critically reflect on their own experiences and assumptions, and could communicate and share what they know.

Although the teachers were aware of the constraints which act against the development of collaborative learning in the classroom (examinations, discipline problems, lack of experience in managing group work) the general view seemed to be that co-operative group work, when successful, could extend the learner's view of the world and develop understanding; furthermore, through collaborative work pupils were enabled to become more articulate, sensitive to others and less competitive.

Observations of actual classroom practice (carried out by teachers on earlier secondments) revealed that the "use of resources was predominantly teacher-directed and administered," that "the worksheet was the main response to the demands of mixed ability teaching" and, in short, that "most learning was teacher-directed." Hence the interest, now, in the commitment of the team of seconded teachers to developing group work across the curriculum. A major task facing the team is to help colleagues to resolve the discrepancy between their wish to change on the one hand and the predominance of knowledge-based didactic teaching on the other. The team, having perceived the wish for change, needs now to create a supportive framework which allows change to happen. By the end of the year of secondment, the team feels cautiously optimistic about the progress which has been made: a climate supportive of planned change is developing. And although there is variation in the extent to which teachers at the school have become committed to these innovative methods, it is felt that many people have gained the confidence to make changes.

In particular the climate for change has developed through the use of team-work involving colleagues from different subjects:

"Teachers who were last year talking in terms of geography, history, RE, SPE are now talking about 'the Humanities team.' They are now very committed to the idea of an area of experience-based curriculum where groups of children are serviced by teams of staff, in many cases interdisciplinary, ie a Humanities team, a creative design team, an expressive arts team. But we need space to develop this further. There's no shortage of good ideas around. There's no shortage of will or commitment. There is a shortage of skills – interpersonal skills in the first place, group skills and the study of group dynamics, how groups operate, under what circumstances, how teams can be put together in such a way that they're balanced." (M2)

The problem, then, has been lack of experience:

"They haven't had the opportunity so the majority of staff still find it difficult to identify what the skills are, how to make them available to other people, how to organise and structure their approach and their methodology in order that children acquire these skills." (M2)

Meanwhile, a team of teachers has been working collaboratively throughout the year to produce materials and ideas for a week-long module on mental handicap. We were able to observe the module in action during the summer term and use it now as a final illustration of how a co-operative venture works in practice.

The mental handicap project

Participation in the Mental Handicap Project, funded by the Mental Health Foundation and MENCAP, resulted in the development of a module about the issues surrounding mental handicap. Second-year pupils worked alongside mentally handicapped children during one week in the summer term on a range of activities including toy design, drama, co-operative games, art and music; the pupils also explored issues (eg prejudice and discrimination; the impact on the family which a mentally handicapped child can have; the educational and emotional needs of mentally handicapped people; factors which cause mental handicap) through discussion, writing a magazine, role-play and other exercises, visits and meetings with parents and other adults involved in the care of mentally handicapped children. Group work was a predominant method throughout the week.

A pack of materials designed by groups of teachers, working in collaboration with a research team at the University, covered aspects of mental handicap such as an historical perspective from Ancient Greece to the present day; a review of the causes of mental handicap; the role of language and communication in particular (eg the uses of the MAKATON sign language system); the effect on the individual of stereotyping and labelling; mental handicap and family life; mental handicap and society.

We observed many informal instances of caring and involvement on the part of the second-year pupils for whom the module was designed. Group work enabled pupils in each class to share attitudes towards mental handicap and experiences of relating to mentally handicapped relatives and acquaintances; they described how the experience of meeting the mentally handicapped children had changed their attitudes ("I used to be scared of them but I'm not now"); they showed awareness of the misconceptions which can arise in relationships with the mentally handicapped: ("You think they're ignoring you and they're not when they don't respond to you and they don't talk back" or "Everyone's prepared for it here in school but in the street some people laugh"); and they expressed empathy for the feelings of the handicapped children:

"Natalie (a child with Down's Syndrome) was crying because the people she knew really well were not there."

"Pam (another child with Down's Syndrome) seemed to be having all these ideas and then when they were asking she said 'I know! I know!' and then they'd be all quiet and she'd just sit there and look at everybody."

"This girl in a wheelchair didn't answer when the lady called her name . . . She might have been shy."

One boy, whose response to a discussion of the genetic causes of Down's Syndrome had been nervous giggling and jeering, changed after taking part in an exercise in which the group had re-labelled everyday objects so that he was confused and appeared incompetent. In talking afterwards about mental handicap, he said:

"Before I'd never met any handicapped people. Doing the exercise felt funny. If you feel funny yourself, you know what they feel like."

To what extent does this kind of module, designed largely for small group work, facilitate a sensitive response to emotions surrounding the issue of mental handicap? Does it increase understanding? Are attitudes changed? A number of teachers complained that "there was a tremendous amount of content to get through" and they "felt under pressure to complete tasks." One example drawn from the first day illustrates such a missed opportunity. During the session on the genetic causes of mental handicap, the teacher asked members of the group to describe the characteristics of children with Down's Syndrome. They clearly did not know how to answer. Some mentioned "something about their eyes", one said "they have large, round faces." One boy suddenly said "I knew an albino boy at my last school." Now although this has nothing to do with Down's Syndrome, the boy was raising a relevant issue about attitudes towards children who are different since he began to describe ways in which this classmate was treated by his peers and the feelings which he must have had. The teacher, anxious about covering the topic of chromosomal abnormality in children with Down's Syndrome, did not feel able, at first, to let this line of discussion develop. But it happened on the first day and later in the week, when the pupils had experienced a variety of experimental workshops, discussion groups, music-making, observation and role-play, teachers found it easier to stop and explore issues as they arose.

We noted that a number of children, in the small group discussions, were able to draw on their own experiences of disabled relatives. For example, one girl described how her cousin had disrupted his family's life to such an extent that his mother had a nervous breakdown; another contrasted this with her cousin's family who have accepted his disability and are happy with him. The personal account of her own experience by the parent of a handicapped child enhanced these discussions and encouraged one group of girls to explore the issue as it might some day apply to themselves as mothers.

Teachers did work collaboratively to produce the materials for the week, but there was a strong feeling by staff that more time should have been allocated to enable the process of cross-fertilisation of ideas through teacher discussion, centred on drafting and editing materials. As a result, some discussion sheets were pitched at an inappropriate level for second-year pupils, (eg Open University handouts on mental handicap and the family); restlessness on the part of the children in some discussion groups needed to be considered in this context. Many sessions, especially at the beginning of the week, were very teacher-centred with teachers not asking for children's views but questioning them about the information on the worksheets and not allowing scope for the children to think. With more time for reflection and planning these difficulties can be overcome, and teachers will also learn to be more accepting of the experiences offered by pupils as a content worth exploring in group discussions.

Again, the key issue is how do staff learn from experience so that they can develop the ways of working that the new content and structures require? Perhaps by sharing their own perceptions in small supportive groups before working with pupils, teachers could have developed greater sensitivity to the issues surrounding mental handicap – such as coping with fear and prejudice. There were several occasions, for example, when teachers seemed unwittingly to invite prejudice rather than to reduce it. One said, almost categorising handicapped people as 'strange', "Down's Syndrome children are different from you. They won't live as long as you." Another, seeing handicap as a 'burden for women' asked, "How would you girls cope with having a handicapped baby?"

Yet the imaginative range of experimental exercises and co-operative learning activities during the week created a warm, accepting atmosphere as the following statements by pupils show:

"They were more intelligent than I thought they were and they were more sensitive."

"I think we should work with them more."

"I thought they might be a bit crazy but they're not. I met a girl called Pam. She didn't want me to leave her."

Comment

This is a school which is committed to group work as part of a wider policy of change. The group work is developing well but in relatively self-contained areas of the curriculum, such as Activities, SPE, the Mental Handicap Project. The task for the Head and the staff is to make links between these strands and the rest of the curriculum and to ensure that teachers and pupils understand more about the principles of group work, and what it can achieve socially and intellectually.

Developing a whole school practice to match a policy is not easy but as the Head says, "We're beginning to grow!"

THE DALE SCHOOL: CO-OPERATING TEACHERS, CO-OPERATING PUPILS

Background

This 11-18 school serves a mixed catchment area on the edge of the city. Some of the pupils come here from the surrounding privately owned houses but the majority travel from the nearby council estate, a short bus-ride away. The school has in the last three years been undergoing a major curriculum review both on its own initiative and in partnership with the LEA through the scheme of school-focused secondments and curriculum panels. As a result of an improved dialogue between subject departments and pastoral teams, a substantial programme of interdisciplinary work has been, and still is being, produced and the impetus for change, which in the past has been largely management-inspired, is gradually shifting to the whole school staff.

The initiative for change grew out of a general concern about the 14-16 curriculum as Hugh, a Deputy Head, explained in a document:

"The staff had expressed an interest in a complete revision of the upper school (14-16) curriculum. At the root of their concern was an evident mismatch between the expectations of staff and pupils. Too few of the latter seemed to have motivation or to enjoy success in the broadest sense of the word. Few of them seemed prepared for the rigours of a strict diet of exam-oriented courses broken up with the weekly helping of PE and community education. These exam courses and the option system . . . dominated both the structure and the content of the final two years of compulsory schooling. All pupils, regardless of ability, were locked into a similar process with only minor adjustments being possible for the less academic. The option system, while trying to equate pupil choice with curriculum balance and timetabling requirements, found too many courses chasing fewer and fewer children as the school faced falling rolls."

The commitment to change was strongly supported by the school's senior management team. Hugh provides a powerful and participatory impetus for change, and the Head, who is as committed but in a quieter way, supports him fully. Hugh is charismatic and has the capacity to make you feel enthusiastic, even elated, when you talk to him about changing the curriculum. His conviction stems from a profound concern about under-privileged pupils that is rooted in political idealism and religious values. Hugh believes that the school must concentrate on developing ways of working that express certain fundamental values – values which, in his view, society is retreating from in its dealing with some of its members:

"The kids will arrive to us in the morning having watched
blue movies the night before on the video. They come into school
and we start talking about co-operative group work and the
value of the individual person. We attack notions of racism
or sexism. (We try to) see different people as of equal value. That is not
the view of our society. So, although I am confident that what we are
doing here is good, it's by no means enough . . . (It's a) competitive,
individualistic society where the individual's concern can be put
above everybody else's . . . As a school we must fight against all of
these things."

A working party of 15 volunteer teachers was formed to make proposals for the reshaping of the 14-16 curriculum. The staff accepted their plan which was based on the idea of a core curriculum (ie compulsory areas of study) with some additional option courses. The core was to occupy 28 periods in a 40 period week with the remaining 12 periods for options. All periods were to be timetabled as doubles. The core curriculum was to consist of three broad areas: maths and science; English and humanities; craft, design and leisure. Integrated courses were to be developed in each of these three areas.

Progress towards an integrated curriculum and towards more active and participatory styles of learning has been greatest in the English/humanities area where a number of 'module-writing groups' have been set up. The Deputy Head himself has worked most intensively for this area, and most members of the original working party that produced the blue print for the core/options scheme also came from this area.

We focus on the developments in this area because not only has group work become a central teaching and learning strategy but the teachers involved have arrived at a shared perception of the importance of group work which they also try to articulate to pupils. Through their obvious commitment to team work and consultation they offer a model of collaboration in action to pupils, and they claim that their understanding is largely shaped by this day to day experience of co-operative group work at their own level.

The main hurdle to be overcome was that of identification with their subjects and teachers acknowledged the need to sacrifice self-interest to group endeavour. Talking and working together exposed differences in attitudes and expectation, and the exploration of these differences enriched and strengthened the team's thinking: "If you come to our meetings, there's a general air of co-operation. Even when there are disagreements, there are enough of us to say 'Well, let's try and ease that one through." Discussions take place in weekly timetabled meetings for each module group and the whole humanities team (15 teachers) meets twice a term. Hugh, the Deputy Head, comments on the importance of staff discussion and co-operation:

"I mean they see that they're never alone, it is a group
decision . . . We're all pulling together, you know, we are like a
big crew together, and there is in a sense no captain but there are a
number of . . . people who have specific roles to play."

The principles he holds for pupils extend to colleagues:

"Individual staff must all feel worth, individual worth in
their place of work, and that is achievable only in a group . . . That
is the success I think of our humanities scheme."

Group work in the humanities area

Hugh explained that teaching in humanities subjects conventionally had an element of group discussion: "You set off the task, the kids do it, and you have group discussion at the end." Discussion, in this structure, involves the whole class in a collaborative review of their work. Hugh and his colleagues moved from this to a situation where pupils were encouraged to co-operate in the process of enquiry itself and not just in the review. He justifies the move in these terms:

"Since the 1960s, teachers who have considered their subject
in the light of the world in which we live have searched for ways
in which kids can share their experiences one with another
and relate what we're trying to deal with in terms of syllabus
to their own life. You don't live by yourself; you seldom work
by yourself; you seldom make decisions by yourself. I mean these
are the ways that we learn as people."

The humanities team sees group work as a way of increasing participation and enjoyment levels. One factor in the success of the approach may, of course, be the teacher's own enthusiasm and growing confidence in managing the shift of role and responsibility that group work requires:

"I love group work providing you're organised. And I think kids love it. I've done it with some first years recently and it was a pretty chaotic lesson. They were all buzzing around doing these plays. God they were buzzing! They loved every minute of it. I couldn't get into the groups, you know, because they didn't want the teacher there. They're buzzing away and organising themselves, ordering people to do this, arguing about things . . . a fantastic education. It doesn't really matter what the end product is."

These teachers assume that learning will be greater when pupils are involved in the learning task and they see group work as offering pupils "some control over their lives . . . It's giving . . . a sense of independence . . . Being able to express their ideas and feel they can actually tackle issues, that things aren't too big for them." This aspiration is expressed particularly in the way teachers relate to pupils in terms of both knowledge and discipline. Take discipline:

"As soon as you've said to another human being "Do this" or you pick someone up by the ear or you're tough and nasty and say, "Now don't you think I'm going to put up with any of that sort of Bla Bla Bla," you've established a relationship and you have established that this is ultimately how you feel about them. And if you then ease up, all you're doing is handing out in a condescending manner to the inferior masses . . . If anything goes wrong I just sit down with them and just talk about why they haven't worked or whatever. But I can't remember the last time I had to raise my voice to a kid. And I think that group work is one of the things that does that because you take the heat off the kid."

"This is another thing that I feel very strongly about, the value of group work. If you're standing at the front of the class you're demanding the attention of all the kids. For those who can't or who won't you're saying, "All right. Knuckle under or flout my authority" in which case I'll have to do something and then you're in a potential conflict situation. If they're working in groups, you go and sit with the kid and you say, "Now then. What have you got here. Oh, haven't you done it? I thought you had done that last week. Oh, I see, well . . ." You know what

I mean. Now it would be a very remarkable kid who stood up and said, "I'm not doing this" wouldn't it? You're more interested in their work than in their subservience."

And knowledge:

"It's important to encourage groups not to seek the answer from the teacher but to seek the answers from each other. . . They're in groups but they still think individually, and so individuals will then ask the teacher and I think that the teacher should be in a position to say, "Don't ask me, ask your group. That is why you are there." There's a transfer of authority from the teacher to the pupils, but to the pupils in small collectives or pairs."

Teachers always try to explain the purpose and principles of group work in terms that pupils will understand:

"I think that when anyone is to achieve anything they have to see the purpose of it. I think it should be laid down for pupils. I did this at the beginning of the year. I said, 'I'm going to be looking at a number of things. Firstly there's these intellectual things but I'm also looking to see how you perform, how you contribute to co-operative work, how you contribute to group decision-making.' I think it's important to appeal to the notion of co-operation and helping each other out, collective responsibility, and actually I think that most kids understand that."

Ways of behaving within the groups are also explained and justified, for principles of active participation and the sharing of responsibility are not ones that pupils readily acquire in conventional classroom settings. They have, therefore, to be legitimised and nurtured:

"I think that in doing this kind of work it is important to emphasise to the pupils repeatedly that *they* have to make decisions and that there are decisions which have to be discussed in a pair or a group and I try to emphasise the notion of group or collective responsibility. (I say to them), "If you want this decision to be recommended on behalf of your group it is in your interest to have actually contributed to arriving at that decision." That's one way of getting over the problem of people riding on the backs of others."

The humanities teachers echo Hugh's view that their own experience of working together co-operatively helps them to understand the difficulties that pupils might face when they are first challenged by the need to work closely with their peers. They are also very sensitive to the benefits of group work for pupils who in conventional class teaching situations often remain distanced and unmotivated. They offer accounts of individual pupils who are often, at first, just as alienated in the new structure but who discover, given time and support, that it is possible to change their habitual ways of behaving:

"One lad doesn't pull his weight in the group. He is a very difficult lad. The other three have worked hard to include him and he is getting better. I think that he has become aware that he doesn't find it easy to talk in groups. Now I think that is useful, because until he actually realises it, there is no way you can start correcting it . . . I think it is probably the first time he has worked for any length of time with a group of people and I think *he* has realised that he has difficulties in relating to other people which was a thing that I knew very clearly . . . Now he is actually relating to the other three. They also learn in trying to help him. I think they were amazingly patient with him. They went out of their way to find things that he could actually cope with without actually saying that they would give him the easy stuff. One thing he is good at is lettering and they gave him lettering so in a subtle way they were managing to include him without actually putting him down."

Another difficult pupil was offered the opportunity to work with a group of four pupils; the teacher's logic was explained to the pupil – who accepted it and joined the group:

"I said, look, how about I put you with this group? I said the big benefit would be that you would be with four people, two of whom are probably the most able people in the year and the other two are very highly motivated, and you know that will help you to work properly. And you know, he said, 'Yes, I'd like that', and he's been fine."

Then there was Mary who was normally a problem in whole-class activity:

"Funny girl, that . . . She's a classic case of the success of group work. That girl was reckoned to be very difficult, she's reckoned to be loudmouthed, to have a difficult, even unpleasant air of familiarity bordering on indiscipline, and seems to have quite a breakdown of relationship with some teachers, and if I was standing at the front of the class spouting . . . and then getting them all to write an essay, I think she'd have cracked, definitely . . . You see her work (now) . . . she's produced more written work mounted than any other kid so far . . . She's certainly got a very nice air

about her now, hasn't she?" (Mary was working on a
letter which she was writing in her role, in the group situation, as
a policeman's wife to a friend in England. Her source was a real-life
account in *Woman's Own* by a Northern Ireland policeman's wife
about what it was like living with a man whose work daily brought
risk to his life.)

Group work in a humanities module: an example

The teacher quoted above was referring to work in a
module on Northern Ireland. The humanities team have so far
completed eight modules of work. Pupils choose, each term, one
from the titles currently available:

Term I: Conflict
             Media Studies
             World Vision

Term II: Work in a Changing World
             People in Cities
             Politics and Political Movements

Term III: Northern Ireland: a Study of Minds
             Body Matters.

Although the titles are very different, the modules
have been developed to a common set of principles which
include: mixed-ability teaching; integration of subjects (English,
history, geography and political/social perspectives); a concern
that issues or themes will provide a clear route through each
module; a concern that assessment and examinations will reflect
and not dominate or distort the learning; and a commitment to
non-didactic methods.

To illustrate group work in action in the humanities area,
we will focus on work in one module: *Northern Ireland: A Study
of Minds*. The module has, as a main objective, the development
in pupils of the capacity to take the perspective of other people,
in particular people whose views differ radically from their own.
The issues to be explored included the social and historical
factors which lead people to have radically differing views, the
varying perceptions which individuals have of the same event,
and the impact on social and personal relationships of different

value systems. The course was seen as not primarily a study of Northern Ireland but rather 'a study of minds.'

Teachers of the module saw themselves as facilitators rather than 'founts of knowledge.' Pupils were encouraged to work in groups, to co-operate and share, to make presentations and to listen to one another, and to take responsibility for their own progress. Each pupil was asked to empathise with one particular role representative of differing perspectives in Northern Ireland – British soldier, Sinn Fein member, UDA member, ordinary Protestant parent, ordinary Catholic parent – and to become thoroughly familar with the historical, personal, social and religious perspectives which such an individual might have had. This empathy was expressed in a number of ways – through writing, drama, poetry, wall-display, presentation of news reports, film-making – and, ultimately, pupils explored ways of understanding roles other than their own through dialogue, debate and discussion with members of other groups. Some pupils also took on the role of impartial mediator between individuals whose views differed radically (eg when 'a British soldier' encountered 'a member of Sinn Fein'); both mediators and discussants had been briefed in the skills of listening and reflecting back.

Each group had a box of attractively prepared materials relevant to the role. These included historical background information, original sources, first-hand accounts of events, case-studies, photographs, letters, newspaper reports, statistics; there were also films and ideas on aspects of the conflict in Northern Ireland. The packs had been compiled by a team of humanities teachers – a historian, a geographer and an English specialist working collaboratively. These teachers met for preliminary discussions, went away and worked individually, and then came back to share and develop ideas and reject material which in the end seemed unsuitable. This process of cross-fertilisation and critical thinking resulted in five packs of highly-organised, challenging materials and exercises. All found it helpful to work with people from other disciplines. As Dorothy, the English teacher, put it:

"I don't think we do nearly enough of group discussions and co-operative preparation of materials. It was very valuable . . . We just don't do it very often in schools. We don't discuss what we're teaching and how we're teaching it and what approach we are using nearly enough, and once something like the treadmill gets going in a school year you don't often step back and do that."

The teachers' collaborative enterprise also modelled the way in which they hoped that the pupils would learn to work. Each had shared areas of expertise, worked through conflicts of interest or perspective, conceded points, even abandoned ideas in the process of working towards shared meanings and mutual understanding. Jon, for example, whose sympathies were essentially with Nationalists in Ireland, said that "the effect of the course on me was to soften my attitude to every group. Although historically I can't support any other side but the Nationalist side, I feel like I have a lot of insight into how an ordinary Protestant feels – just about the opposite to what I emotionally feel! And I'm hoping there will be that effect on the kids." Could the pupils engage in a similar learning process in the course of coming to terms with complex and conflicting ideas about Northern Ireland? Jon was sure that they could, and that an important aspect was the responsibility which the pupils took for their own learning:

"I think it's particularly important in humanities. If we want to do an exposition on 19th century Irish history obviously I'm going to produce the best one in the class for the purely logistic reason that I've been studying it longer. I am more expert than them. But in the context of classrooms, my view is not more valid than a kid's view, providing it's a reasonably informed view and not just a blind one, and providing we give them enough information to make a rational judgment and get them involved enough in it. That's what this process is all about."

How did the pupils experience the module? We saw many examples of young people helping one another and working collaboratively to understand the complexities of life in Northern Ireland. We saw enjoyment and enthusiasm and a tolerance for people who needed help. We also saw instances of growth from prejudice to understanding. Even one very withdrawn girl, who had great difficulty in becoming involved in any group, evoked sympathetic and tolerant responses from other group members who were able to empathise with her problems and understand destructive behaviour on her part.

The pupils clearly felt at ease when they were given the opportunity to express ideas to a small group of peers. "You're not frightened to ask questions of people in your own age group" was how one girl expressed it. This meant that the classroom atmosphere was relaxed and informal but that there was also a high level of involvement in the group tasks. They also appreciated the fact that their teacher "joins in with you" and "sits with your group and talks"; they felt that they were being taken seriously and responded positively as a result.

The teachers indicated that they had fewer discipline problems in this context. They suggested that group work actually makes control easier for the teacher "since the individuals seemed to develop responsibility towards their group." In fact, as one teacher put it, "kids seem to develop an enthusiasm which at times transcends normal expectations of pupil involvement in the classroom." The dynamics of the group generated a sense of excitement. "When we're working together it clicks!" "Yes, you get more ideas from other people" and "If you're just sat on your own and you think 'Oh no! I don't know what to do, do I?' that's the worst one. That's one that gets nearly everybody. 'What shall I do?' If other people are there they give you ideas, they help you generate your own ideas."

Pupils seemed to welcome the chance to explore a range of perspectives:

"Last year you had to do what teacher told you, and everybody did the same thing, whereas this time you're all doing different. You see all different sides of the story."

"I think that if you sat down with a text book you'd think, 'Oh God, I've got to learn it again'. But this way it's like research."

"Everybody's there for you but you've got to find it. It makes you want to do it. It's a good way of doing things!"

It was also interesting to consider the types of criticism which some pupils levelled at the module. One boy expressed concern that he was getting a slanted picture of Ireland by taking on the role of a Protestant extremist. He said, "What we should have done is done a lot of work on *all* things and then picked out which one we wanted to do. So that at least we knew what were going on in the other half." Yet at the same time he showed that he *was* developing a critical capacity in interpreting information. For one thing, he pointed out the need to use primary sources:

"You should ask someone who's actually experienced it,
instead of using booklets and secondary sources."

(He drew a parallel with our method of finding out about
group work in The Dale School by using interview data.) His
friend disagreed and pointed to bias in news reports:
"It's like with the miners' strike, everyone were on the
police's side weren't they?"

He added:
"That's what we're looking at. We're in England, aren't we,
now? We're looking at papers and news reports. That's all you can
get about Northern Ireland . . . In a way this course has opened up
us eyes an awful lot."

This module illustrates a most effective way of using
group work in the classroom. We would suggest that certain key
ingredients guaranteed its success. For one thing, the materials
were thoroughly researched by the course team. This meant that
the pupils were presented at the beginning of the module with
a clear outline of what they were expected to do and what the
overall aims of the course were. The packs gave structured tasks
for pupils to do, many in a group setting; they were also open to
change and modification in the light of experience.

Classes were timetabled to take place at the same time
so that staff could continue to collaborate during the teaching of
the module. This arrangement made possible a greater flexibility
of grouping and gave scope for visiting speakers, an exhibition
of photographs, videotaping, etc. There was a strong sense that
the course was on-going and that the materials would continue
to evolve with time.

The course was about perspective-taking both in Northern
Ireland (or any other country in conflict) and within the
classroom itself. The teachers recognised the need to set aside
time to evaluate the learning processes as they happened. This
kind of reflection did not come very easily at first, but the
pupils became more familiar with self-reflection as the module
progressed. Perhaps this area is the most difficult and one where
most anxiety can be felt. As Dorothy said:
"It's very easy to abandon these things because, when you
see kids stuttering and giggling, and other kids making comments,
it's very easy to think that doesn't work. But if you do stick at it,
they do get better."

The structured debriefing exercises (eg where pupils encountered one another in role with a mediator present) led to the most successful outcomes in terms of concentration and capacity to listen to another person't point of view.

Finally, the most powerful illustration of the learning which had taken place emerged at the University some weeks after the module ended when 20 pupils demonstrated the materials to a group of teachers on secondment. They showed knowledge of the issues in Northern Ireland, displayed confidence in putting forward points of view, and took on the role of facilitators in helping the adults to try out some of the exercises:

"It strikes me as one of the most important things we
should be developing with teaching people the joy of working
together . . . It's the electricity of learning other people's
ideas!"

Group work outside the humanities area

Before embarking on the humanities programme, pupils have probably not had any sustained experience of group work. As they come to see group work as a legitimate way of learning, and an important way of learning, they are more likely to accept it in other areas of the curriculum. But at the moment the reluctance to develop group work outside the humanities area seems in fact to lie more with the teachers than with the pupils. There are several reasons for this: in the humanities area teachers feel that co-operative, discussion-based learning fits naturally with the content and image of the subject; second, the mutual support for change that the humanities team members provide for each other is important; third, the experience of learning to work co-operatively together at the teacher's own level seems to have yielded a further degree of commitment and appreciation; fourth, the Deputy Head, whose own values support the development of learning strategies based on group work, has given a lot of active support to the teachers in this area.

Moreover, the teachers' readiness to work in an integrated way may be stronger – according to a science teacher – because the humanities teachers teach their 'subjects' elsewhere in the school. In their subject-based teaching they might not, he thinks, be so ready to introduce group work because they too would have some uncertainties as to whether the same level of intellectual achievements could be met. But in the new 14-16 modular programme, other things are being assessed – "making things interesting, lively, active, demanding" – and traditional learning outcomes as such are less prominent. At the same time, the science teacher sees this as a useful preliminary strategy: teachers might gain confidence in their integrated work to introduce group methods and other forms of active learning into their subject based work.

Pat, one of the two science teachers we interviewed, said that his department was "not in the vanguard of change." He was very committed to group work but only found an opportunity to do it outside science teaching – in the integrated environmental studies course where he worked with the Head of Special Needs! "The situation in science is so slow to change. I'm not prepared to sit around and wait for that . . . so I've tried elsewhere." He saw this opportunity as important but limited: "We've been exploring styles of group work that are not necessarily compatible with academic ends and objectives." He thinks that a necessary condition for developing different ways of learning in science is "willingness amongst colleagues . . . to take on board new experiences." But in science, compared with the humanities area, you've got "a different group of people – and you have to explore with people what their interests, fears, their concerns, their strengths, their weaknesses are."

There has been no tradition of such exchange among science teachers. Why this reserve? First of course is the weight of the assumptions about science that are built into the structure of school science – relating particularly to the importance of a factual base, to the need for 'certainties' and about the sequences and structures of learning. Secondly, there is the false defence of the claim: "We're doing it already." In fact it is often a lack of equipment that forces pupils to work in pairs on experiments. The principles of group work do not necessarily inform paired work unless the teacher has explored with pupils how they can make the most of the opportunity to work effectively together. Third, even with the support for group work that GCSE claims to give, the examination still seems, in Pat's view, to endorse a traditional view of science. The way through to colleagues, as he sees it, is motivation: if they can observe and experience the excitement of seeing "kids get on with one another without constraint and see them actually get some joy out of doing that," then they may come to commit themselves to exploring a different teaching strategy in their mainstream science teaching. At present, Pat argues, the science curriculum serves best only those pupils who wish to study science to a high level.

Pat's view is that the need for a change of strategy is most acute in science teaching and he sees the way forward as being through the legitimisation of exploring controversial social issues in science using discussion-based group work.

As we have seen, one of Pat's explanations of the lack of opportunity to develop group work in the science/maths area was the absence of a common commitment among the staff. Certainly Ray, the other science teacher whom we interviewed, saw things in more traditional terms. He expressed anxieties about group work that a lot of teachers seem to be troubled by and that are therefore worth quoting. He asked whether in group work "you get a couple of people doing nothing." (But, we wondered, don't a lot "do nothing" in the sense of not thinking for themselves in most lessons?) He also said that if groups are large then some pupils will "sit on the sidelines and get into mischief." (But, we thought, isn't the teacher able to control the size and composition of the group?) And yet Ray is not content with the situation as it exists at present:

"If I'm in the middle, I tend to be holding court, which isn't very good because I talk and one other pupil talks and then another and then another and maybe quite a few people don't contribute anything to that discussion."

We asked what held him back from occasionally splitting pupils up into small groups to have a discussion on some aspect of the work so that they could all make a contribution. He commented:

"I don't know. Perhaps because you get set in your ways and always do things that way and you carry on doing it that way and of course that's not always the best way of doing things. I think I have more control over things (in the traditional situation). I'm not particularly extrovert. I find it very difficult to go through role play in this sort of group activity and so I tend to steer clear of that kind of thing. I don't feel it's me. I would need a few drinks first before I'd feel happy doing that sort of thing."

Ray has three fairly widely held misconceptions of group work. First, that it is mainly about role play (this may be a view that he has taken from hearing Pat talk about group work). Second, that in group work the teacher has to be an extrovert. Third, that for a discussion in science, pupils need to have a large and systematically-constructed body of facts at their disposal:

"I think there are things that come from group work, from people interacting, hearing other people's opinions and ideas, possibly modifying their own opinions and prejudices by hearing them but . . . well I can see that it's useful . . . I think that for discussion work people need the facts first. They would need to be given a body of knowledge first. Having opinions isn't much good unless they're based on a body of facts ."

And so Ray stays with the familiar, but he realizes that the familiar does not serve the majority of his pupils:

"Having said that, the exam isn't always going to be of much use to those pupils who pass it . . . It might well be that if we did spend more time discussing things in groups that their actual maturity and general approach to adults would be very much better and might stand them in good stead in the world of work."

What seems to be at stake is whether group work can actually deliver in terms of intellectual achievement in science. Is it only about processes of social enquiry? Uncertain how to move, and uncertain as to whether a move is legitimate in science, Ray manages to suppress his anxieties about the way he currently works. He needs the support of others, both in and outside the school. At present, alternative teaching methods "are not put forward as being the way forward" by those whose views he respects in science teaching. A small source of satisfaction is that he feels able to introduce some discussion work into his sixth form groups – but here again only a minority of pupils will have the opportunity to see science, as Kuhn saw it, as about crucial shifts of paradigm and as controversial in its social applications:

"Lower down the school we tend not to cloud the issues with distractors which may lead to insecurity or uncertainty about things. We scientists tend to suggest that what we teach is right. I think that, to a certain extent, there is reassurance in knowing that you've done this particular piece of work, you've got

67

this result, and it's right . . . I feel that the things that I'm teaching in physics are very much certainties."

Pat is perhaps too junior a colleague to provide the vision that other science teachers will follow and the security of a formal policy that others could refer to. And in any case his view of group work is expressed in terms that are likely to deter rather than to reassure colleagues who are nervous about their own competence to handle group work and are seeking evidence of its capacity to achieve academic as well as process skills.

In one of the new core curriculum areas, the scientists are joined by the mathematicians. We interviewed only one mathematician. Asked about group work, he said categorically "I never work in that way and I don't think anyone else in the department does." Where the SMP programme is followed, pupils are working on their own and only rarely is there any activity that involves more than one person. Like Ray, Clive and his colleagues have anxieties that stem from personal and professional uncertainty:

"I think these doubts stem from our own ignorance – what
we're doing it for, how to do it and how to make it effective. When
you're using a new method I think you've got to spend some
time getting used to it in order to realize its potential."

He did not reject the idea, however, that group work can be done in maths:

"I think that maths is just like any other subject. A lot of
the concepts that we're dealing with in maths for the average pupil
are difficult to understand and I think that with discussion this in
fact helps them to understand . . . I think that looking at things in
different ways, doing things in different ways and getting
other people's views is useful . . . I think that sometimes the pupil
who has grasped a problem can help another pupil as easily as I
can or maybe even better because they maybe think along the
same wave lengths . . . It also gives them confidence to be able to
communicate ideas to someone else. It makes me put into words
how I understand the idea and by doing that I think it helps me to
understand something about it and I think the same thing can happen
to the pupils."

Clive does not think it easy for people in a departmental structure who have been working together for some time to initiate any radical change of direction. Evidence of this is the time that maths teachers have already spent on thinking about problem-solving and investigatory work, and yet these approaches have still not been built in as a central policy. He feels that some concerted push from a sympathetic outsider is needed in order to make a group of people move. This may be what happened in the humanities area when the Deputy Head came to work alongside the teachers in the teams. Clive also points to the need for individuals to recognise the basis of their own commitment to change. "To be honest," he says, "group work hasn't come far enough up my list of priorities to put enough energy into it." His colleagues, he feels, "are waiting" for something to energize them and give them a coherent commitment. Although some seeds have been sown, "we are not yet at the stage of seeing a major growth from our seeds. Maybe we could do it if there was a bit of enthusiasm."

In this new curriculum area, comprising two weighty traditional subjects, a lot of thought will need to be given to ways of managing change if individual concerns, often unarticulated, about the adequacy of present teaching methods are to be voiced in a common forum. Teachers will need support in confronting publicly what they sometimes face in the privacy of the interview, namely, that much of what they do has little long-term value for the majority of the pupils they teach.

In this study, we concentrated on those two of the three core curriculum areas that brought together subjects that have traditionally been seen as academic, for it is in these subjects that it is usually more difficult to introduce and sustain changes of teaching style. The third core curriculum area was called "craft, design and leisure" and included teachers of CDT and home economics. Home economics of course has classrooms that, in recent years, have been designed with peninsular bases that support group work. In CDT however there is often a strong tradition of individual activity. How far has the idea of group work developed in this new core curriculum area in the Dale School?

The Head of CDT, Mike, has an industrial orientation and values the importance of learning to co-operate in groups in order to excel in competition with other groups. He believes it important that pupils are helped to understand how output is related to group process:

"You get an example, a group doing too much talking and
not producing much. Well that's a good example for showing the
kids how a firm can go broke by the fact that it's bought too much
and not produced anything . . . It's a good model for showing them
how industry works and it helps them to work in a group."

Group work offers an arena for "healthy" competition
in that pupils are not competing against each other in
personal, individual terms. Individual failure is therefore not
underlined as it often is in traditional classroom activity.
As with teachers in the humanities area, Mike believes in
explaining the principles of group work to the pupils:

"You've got to tell them about the maintenance of groups . . .
That we don't want any passengers, we don't want a big boss, we
want them to be a group and decide and carry on. You do get some
that are so democratic that they don't produce anything but you get
others where the leader says you do that or you do this and they get
quite truculent about that. At the end of each lesson I try to leave
enough time to go round and talk about each task, how they've
actually performed, very briefly. I suppose I could actually give them
a questionnaire to reflect on how they operated within the group."

He also believes, as do the humanities teachers, that
group work becomes more acceptable to pupils if they see staff
modelling the approach. He describes pupils' reaction to seeing
four members of staff co-operating over mixing concrete:

"Now this was a revelation for the kids, to see four members
of staff working together, because they see us as individuals. . . . They
saw that we were not arguing and that we were working
co-operatively and that was a good spin-off."

Interestingly, Mike perceives the complexity of group
work without being deterred by it:

"Teaching groups is the most difficult way of teaching
because if you don't know what you're doing and you don't know
what to look for as a teacher, you don't know what to say to the
kids when they get into group dynamics, then you could be putting
your head into the lion's mouth. Things can happen in groups which
create emotion and if it gets out of hand . . ."

He says that people need training in group work and that
it isn't something that you can just "pick up". However, while
the Head of CDT clearly has a commitment to group work, and
a confident experience of it, he is not as yet sharing that experi-

ence in ways which would allow colleagues in the new core curriculum area to explore the possibility of using group work as a central teaching and learning strategy.

Review

What can be learned from the rate of progress towards change in the humanities area? First, as Pat pointed out, the new integrated modules provide an arena for experiment, a test bed for new ideas and approaches which might later be carried into other, more subject-dominated areas of teachers' work. If they are to make fundamental changes to their teaching strategy, teachers need to feel confident about a new approach. The modular curriculum, which is not too much at the mercy of the public examination system, allows humanities teachers to gain confidence in the process of enquiry-based group work. Once they have confidence in their mastery of the process, and some evidence of its effectiveness, then they may be in a position later to evaluate the effectiveness of the approach in relation to more subject-based aims and objectives. What science and maths teachers were unnerved by was the absence, in their own present experience, of any evidence that group work could deliver in conventional learning terms – even though at the same time they are also questioning whether they are right to pursue those conventional learning goals if they show little success in engaging the interest of the majority of the pupils.

Second, we also see the importance of collaboration at the staff level. Staff in the humanities team were able to experience group work at their own level and therefore had a first-hand capacity to appreciate its problems and its possibilities. It is also helpful if pupils see that a way of working is important because teachers are working in this way. The existence of a staff group as a reference point is significant in embarking on any risky enterprise: the individual is more likely to be courageous if others are known to be taking similar risks and if the experience of uncertainty and even adversity or failure can be shared and used as a basis for learning and recommitment. It is usually much easier to change a group than it is a set of individuals.

Third, in terms of the process of change itself, the humanities team was helped by the fact that a number of its own members had worked together on the school's original working party and had therefore thought through the principles that were to guide the new practices for the school. They therefore had a head start in leading collaborative thinking in the humanities area. Moreover, they had the enthusiastic companionship of the Deputy Head who was himself committed to principles of active learning and collaborative group work.

Fourth, the humanities team explicitly faced the fact that it was engaged in an experiment and that it was taking risks. It therefore made time for continuing discussion for members of module teams and for the whole humanities team. Staff were open about disagreements and indeed saw disagreements, in group activity, as a way of gathering the advantage of different perspectives. They faced the problem of inertia on the part of some colleagues and were not afraid to review the power of the humanities team in relation to the school's staff as a whole. They also came to respect pupils enough to see the need to share with them the procedural principles that were giving coherence and unity to the humanities team's own negotiations.

What kind of intervention might make it possible for teachers in the other two core-curriculum areas to embark on a similar programme of careful and professionally responsible experiment? We hoped that their reading of this study might provide an occasion for their reviewing fairly openly the problems of change in their respective areas, and for their devising strategies which they might be able to commit themselves to pursuing together.

CLASSROOM STUDIES

INTRODUCTION

In this section we offer some accounts of ways in which group work has been developed in particular classroom settings. Each study was chosen to illustrate a different aspect and to highlight learning processes which group work can facilitate. In *Them Stripes*, we focus on the role of group work in helping pupils to develop their powers of criticism; the context is the art lesson, but the principle can be applied to any area of the curriculum where pupils are engaged in forming judgments and developing a vocabulary of criticism. The second classroom study is a longer analysis of group work within the English Department of a multi-cultural school. Here we see how one group of teachers is using collaborative learning methods as a means of helping their pupils to express their own ideas in ways which are meaningful to them. The multi-ethnic classroom highlights the role which co-operative group work can have in forming links between academic learning processes and personal relationships within the class. The third and fourth studies illustrate the use of role play and simulation in coming to understand complex ideas, learning about a range of perspectives and working co-operatively towards a group goal. In each we see pupils working together with great enjoyment as they come to grips with controversial and challenging issues.

"THEM STRIPES": THE DEVELOPMENT OF
CONSTRUCTIVE CRITICISM

In a middle school

Our interest in helping pupils develop a capacity for constructive criticism of their own work and the work of others began with an art teacher in a middle school in East Anglia.

The teacher, Ian, came new to the school and brought with him some innovative ideas about opening up the process of assessment. He rejected the conventional approach where the teacher's judgment is conveyed as a grade, supported by only a brief comment, and where the ways of looking that inform the teacher's judgment remain unarticulated. He thought it important that pupils should be helped to understand the criteria by which, for example, an athlete might judge whether he has made a good jump, or an artist might judge the quality of a painting, or a scientist might judge the quality of an explanatory model. Rarely is time consciously spent in schools on helping pupils to discuss criteria and refine judgment through dialogue; pupils may not develop a language that will allow them, as adults, to sustain sensitive discussions of the quality of events or objects. This is probably most likely to happen in relation to sport where public commentaries, relayed through the media, help to build up a common vocabulary for the judgment of form.

Ian tried to develop his ideas by working through written or spoken dialogue between pupil and teacher. His strategy was to ask each pupil to keep a record book in which he or she had to write the dates when a piece of work was started and completed, a title, a commentary, and the grade they thought the work deserved. Ian then added his own commentary and gave the work a grade. If there was a substantial discrepancy, he would move from written dialogue to a discussion of the differences between the way he had looked at and judged the pupil's work, and the way the pupil had looked at it and judged it.

Pupils who had been in the school for one or two years prior to Ian's appointment had difficulty in writing analytic comments. They offered short 'teacher-like' judgments - for example "It was quite good" or "It was a good effort." In contrast the first year pupils, who had not been socialized into accepting the restricted language of conventional assessment, started writing interesting descriptive comments. See for example this response:

"In my picture I use paints and sometimes I mixed colours.
The thing that happened to me was that I was just getting into bed
when I saw spots on my leg. I asked my mum what they were. She
said they were chicken pox. The next morning I had even more spots.
The picture I drew and painted had a green and blue bed and a window
and blue curtains. I had in my picture a dressing table
which was brown."

In time, the model provided by the art teacher's careful analytic comments started to influence the way the pupils looked at and thought about their work. Here is an interesting transitional comment from a younger pupil which shows the narrative/descriptive comment giving way to the analytic:

"My picture is about when I was flying a World War I German
fighter and got shot down on an island where dinosaurs still live. The
brown doesn't show up much with the red but you can see what it
is. The paints have gone runny and gone where I didn't want
them to go. I enjoyed doing the picture very much. I think
that I cannot do any better than that picture which I had just done."

We thought there was potential in this idea, which, if it were developed systematically, could help pupils feel comfortable about making judgments and about understanding judgments made by their teachers. It did not, however, lead to group discussion of criteria. For this, we look at work done by Cathy, an art teacher in a comprehensive school in Sheffield.

In a secondary school

Cathy wanted to encourage her fifth year pupils to discuss criteria for judgment in art. The pupils had had no experience in their earlier years of schooling of such discussions and she decided to use the public examination in art as a motivating force. It turned out that the examination focus was in many ways a constraint, but her experience enabled us to see how her intentions could be more fully and richly realized.

Cathy started by displaying work from the previous year's examinations: for each of the eight examination grades the work of one pupil who had been awarded that grade was displayed on the classroom walls. The pupils could therefore begin to think about what kinds of qualities were securing particular grades. Cathy then asked the pupils to grade four different portfolios of art work. In making their judgments, she asked them to think about such things as colour, texture and shape. This was a promising start but instead of opening up the process by encouraging discussion of the criteria the pupils were using in making their judgments and assigning their grades, she moved them towards a computational exercise in aggregating and manipulating the grades they had given. At the same time she told the pupils that judgment is something that the examiners arrive at through discussion of particular pieces of work. The idea that examiners might disagree was a new one to the class. While the exercise had a useful demystifying and humanising effect, it may have added to some pupils' anxiety about the reliability of the grade that their work would be given when it was submitted for the examination later in the academic year!

We discussed our observations of the lesson with Cathy and she quickly saw the potential of shifting the focus on to group discussion of the work being looked at. She agreed to give pupils an opportunity for such discussion in the next art lesson. Accordingly, next week, she asked every pupil to set out his or her work, and urged pupils to move round the room in small groups discussing how they would judge the work that was in front of them.

Organisationally, the situation was informal and fluid and, with the wisdom of hindsight, we all felt that a more structured approach might have helped, with evenly-sized small groups of three or four pupils, sitting together at a table, concentrating on one portfolio, and then possibly swopping their portfolio with another group and comparing their evaluations. It might have been helpful for the teacher to model ways of looking and talking, perhaps by bringing in some of her own painting and showing them how she would look at and judge her work.

As the pupils moved round the tables of work, we were able to tape-record their comments on what they saw. They were not used to talking about art and found it difficult both to criticise their own work and to offer constructive criticism of each others' efforts. But there was evidence that with regular opportunities for such discussion, they could become interested, confident and thoughtful critics. The impulse to find words to express personal responses was clearly there:

"Neatness . . . textures, shading, something like that. The textures she's using are good. I don't know whether she's using shading or pencil. It's all I can say. I'm not really good at textures." (Pupil)

"Texture and shading. Good drawing. The painting's good. It's neat. The colours are good. They all stand out against one another. They don't cover up one another." (Pupil)

"I like this shape here and that pattern the way she shades it and blends it in. It's colourful. I like it. It's blended dark bits and light bits." (Pupil)

From the tape recordings we learned what things pupils found difficult about their task. For example, there was some embarrassment: as one pupil explained: "It's 'orrible commenting on someone's work when they're stood there listening to you." There was also some evidence that pupils could feel competitive about their own work in a group situation. One pupil said that he would "try to do better than everybody" in the group, and others were nervous lest their ideas might be "stolen" by other pupils.

Some pupils allowed personal feelings about a fellow pupil to influence their judgement of his or her art work. For example, we noticed that one boy was much harder on another boy's drawing one week than he had been the week before and we asked why this was so. He replied: "I hate him now." His mate whispered to us, in explanation: "He's nicked 'is bird." In developing critically constructive peer discussion as a regular feature of the art lessons, Cathy and her colleagues would clearly need to help pupils distance personal and professional feelings; feel confident about contributing to the discussion; help them believe that what they had to say would be listened to; and help them respect and value what other pupils in the class might have to say about their own work.

Our recordings suggested that the most fundamental problem was that the pupils' language for talking about art was limited.

Interviewer Do you ever go to Art Galleries?

Girl *Yes, me and my friend went to the Mappin. We saw pictures . . . you know - them stripes.*

Interviewer Stripes?

Girl *Yes, they were big pictures all in stripes.*

Interviewer (Suddenly it dawns on her) - Oh, you mean Bridget Riley's exhibition?
Girl *Yes, that was her name.*

Where does the vocabulary of art come from we wondered? As we listened to the pupils' responses to the drawings and paintings we kept nudging gently with questions to try to encourage them to find words to describe what they were thinking and feeling:

Pupil *It's fantastic.*
Interviewer Can you get behind saying it's good and fantastic?
Pupil 1 *That doll - the shading on it. It looks as though it's actually there.*
Pupil 2 *You can tell how much time she's taken. The colours!*
Interviewer Is it just a lot of colour that's important?
Pupil 1 *No, not really. It's just how she's used the colours. She's not mixed different colours that don't go together.*

Qualities that pupils felt confident about rating highly included originality (ie not doing the same as everyone else in the class), hard work (ie not using short cuts such as filling in banks of colour with a felt tip rather than with a paint brush) and being realistic (eg "look at lamp post by side of t'wall – it's all out of perspective"). It was understandably more difficult for them to find words to communicate responses that were less technical.

Pupils tended to focus on the product alone and did not take into account the intention – unless they were talking about their own work. They would sometimes dismiss a particular feature with scorn – "It's got a blue leg!" – without considering whether the problem lay in the pupil's vision, the execution, or in their own too conventional expectations and ways of seeing. We were intrigued by the problem of encouraging pupils to explore and compare different perspectives, including the perspective of the viewer and the perspective of the painter. We asked one pair of pupils to comment on a painting of a leaf and then asked the pupil who had painted it to comment. The juxtaposition of the views could have been interesting had the 'critics' and the 'artist' been in the same group:

Pupil 1 *I like that one. It didn't look pastel. I don't know*

what it was done from. It looks all even, all one colour, ap.
the red bits.

Pupil 2 *From a distance it looks as if it were sewn . . . It*
looks like pastel.

Interviewer That's probably why you get that lovely soft
effect.

The girl who painted it said this of it:

"Actually for this one I just did the black and white bits first
and then I was watching a horror film on TV and there was lots of
blood in it and I thought I'll do those bits in red."

The mood of the painting seemed to change when we heard
what had influenced it!

With more opportunities to discuss art works, pupils
could, we think, gain confidence in looking at and talking
about their own work, and the work of their peers, and works
by reputable artists.

Comment

In conclusion, it seems worthwhile to try to relate
the initiatives taken by Ian and Cathy to a project sponsored
by the Schools Council in the early 1980s and called Critical
Studies in Art Education. The project was prompted by concern
that the emphasis on practical work had become so dominant
in art classrooms that contemplation and communication had
virtually disappeared. It was acknowledged that practical activity
alone would not necessarily lead to critical awareness, and that
opportunities had to be created to help pupils become critically
aware, to develop a critical vocabulary, and to become skilled in
discussing responses to art.

The project focused in particular on pupils' experiences as
they started to write or talk about works of art that they had seen.
Pupils were encouraged to look, to talk, and often to make their
own creative response to these art works. The project underlines
the need for a good balance to be maintained between the use of
commonly understood technical words which identify processes
or types of art work, and the personalised language which
supports the expression of individual perception and insight. A
nine year old's comments are quoted to suggest how naturally a
child can combine newly learned technical words with a natural

warmth for the animals and birds depicted in the sculptures which the child had tried to reproduce:

"I liked the duck because it was a good sculpting . . . It was made of alabaster so it was a hard colour to get when I painted it. Alabaster is a translucent stone-like quartz and marble. It has other colours too. I also like Billy the pig who was a runt. Ted (the sculptor) looked after Billy and fed him on goat's milk because cow's milk kills baby pigs. Billy was made of acacia wood and it is a fawn colour. I made a model of Billy."

The project does not offer much evidence of the difficulties of developing group conversation about art, but it does offer a few interesting ideas for stimulating discussion. For example, a painting is described by the teacher, and all pupils in the class draw or paint what they have heard. They then discuss their various interpretations alongside the original painting. A variation on this approach focuses more on small group activity. Pupils are divided into groups of three or four, and one pupil from each group chooses a reproduction from a resource collection (of post cards of works of art) and describes it to the other members of their small group. The other pupils, as before, paint or draw according to the description, and then there is a discussion based on comparisons of the group members' responses both with each other and with the original.

After looking at Ian's and Cathy's initiatives, and after reviewing the work of the Schools Council Project, we concluded that there was considerable scope for teachers to develop, in their own classrooms, ways of helping pupils use group work as a means of developing a habit of constructive critique.

GROUP WORK IN A MULTICULTURAL CONTEXT: HELPING YOUNG PEOPLE TO FIND A VOICE

Introduction

It is a fundamental principle which underlies the use of co-operative learning methods in schools that when people help one another and join together to achieve a common goal they are likely to end up feeling more positively about each other and working more effectively together. (The early work of Sherif and Sherif (1956) demonstrated this in their classic study of conflict and co-operation between rival groups of children at a summer camp.) Instead of separating academic learning and personal relationships, teachers who are committed to co-operative learning methods discover how productively the two can interact. And as Sharan (1985) points out in his chapter on co-operative learning in the multi-ethnic classroom, "when the class is comprised of pupils from different ethnic, racial, or cultural backgrounds, these processes and relationships suddenly assume for teachers a degree of salience that they might not have had when all the students were from the same social group" (p.255). The challenge of the multi-ethnic classroom can highlight for teachers the value of collaborative learning strategies in developing positive relationships and a productive working climate amongst the students.

These ideas are confirmed in the growing literature on co-operative learning processes which also documents important implications for teachers who work in this way. Johnson and Johnson (1985), for example, in their analysis of the processes which mediate between co-operative learning experiences and productivity and interpersonal relationships among students conclude that:

- co-operative procedures may be used successfully with any type of academic task;
- where possible, co-operative groups should be structured so that controversy among group members is possible and is managed constructively;
- students should be encouraged to keep each other on task;
- students should be encouraged to support each other's

efforts to achieve, to give each other feed-back and to ensure that all members are involved in the learning process;

• positive feelings of acceptance and support should be encouraged.

The teachers in this study were positive in their approach to group work and in their belief that it was beneficial to pupils in talking to one another, as well as in deepening understanding of concepts and developing perspective-taking skills. But discipline problems, noise levels, perceptions by colleagues and pupils that it was not real work, lack of space, time and resources were amongst the factors which contributed to the difficulty of organising group work, however much the teachers believed it to be a productive approach to learning.

Furthermore, in the multi-cultural setting there were additional issues to be considered, largely arising from the contrasting values and expectations of the different cultural groups. It may be helpful then to report the study by Sharan et al (1985), who introduced co-operative learning methods into an Israeli junior high school where there were two major ethnic groups – Jews who had emigrated from Muslim countries of the Middle East, Asia and North Africa; and those who came from Europe and America. The teachers experienced a great deal of stress through lack of preplanned lessons and group-work materials. Despite great difficulties in the early stages, the eventual outcomes demonstrated conclusively that co-operative learning in small groups improved communication skills, promoted co-operative, cross-ethnic behaviour amongst pupils in multi-ethnic classrooms, and resulted in greater academic achievement. Slavin's (1983) extensive work in the US on techniques and strategies for co-operative learning also gives teachers new methods for effectively reducing prejudice, promoting pro-social behaviour and encouraging academic achievement in multi-ethnic settings.

In our case study we explore a number of themes. Firstly we look at group work as a means of helping to develop what Sharan calls "equal coexistence and mutual respect among pupils from different ethnic groups." We suggest that group work offers a constructive means of fostering the capacity to understand other people's perspectives without losing one's own sense of identity. (Secondly, we explore the role which group work has in building on good social relationships in order to create an environment in which pupils can work effectively together. Thirdly, we focus on one example of group work in action – the production of a class magazine – where we discuss the extent to which young people can use the group to make articulate their own needs and wishes, we call this "finding a voice."

The school
Forty per cent of the pupil population at the Ainsworth School is black. The school is interested in group work which it is developing in various settings. The Head suggested that I focus on the English Department because he thought that group work was so far most fully developed and actively pursued there and that the teachers had a theory of group work that was well integrated with practice. The acting head of the English Department (his colleague is on a year's secondment) is currently carrying out research for a PhD: his original focus on patois has developed into a much wider involvement in Afro-Caribbean culture. There is a good working atmosphere in the Department. The English team works closely together and, as the Head claimed, they do indeed share a similar philosophy. They all agreed to talk to me about group work in a multi-cultural setting, invited me into their classes and gave me permission to talk freely with pupils.

In a multi-cultural context issues of race, gender and learning are closely inter-related. For example, because of home responsibilities and the likelihood of an early marriage, many Asian girls are not motivated to succeed academically. Also the context is much more complicated than many teachers might think. A teacher acknowledges his surprise at the behaviour of some of the Asian girls in school:

"I expected them to be very good and hard-working and disciplined but they weren't, and it seems maybe some of them are living a double life . . . Perhaps this is the only time they can let their hair down, because some of them are a bit naughty."

He continues:

"A lot of the kids live two different lives. They come here and they're an English kid at school. Then they go home. It's different values and parents expect different conduct from them. It's definitely one of the things about being split between two cultures. Definitely!"

Pupils themselves may experience a conflict of cultural values. One Asian girl describes her experience of conflicting cultural values:

"We've got a teacher from Pakistan. He don't realise how kids are in this country compared to there. He expects us to be just as obedient as people in Pakistan. He says, 'Keep quiet!' and expects the whole class to just shut up and listen to him."

Loyalties can be divided:

"If someone's picking on a Pakistani you don't know whether to side with the person you know or the person that's your own colour." (Asian girl)

"If it's your best friend and she's had an argument with somebody that you know and a Pakistani person expects you to stick up for them because you're Pakistani and your friend expects you to stick up for them that's when you're left in the middle with nowhere to turn to." (Asian girl)

And there are problems of identity:

"Somebody expects us to tell them about our religion or why we do certain things. I think some Pakistanis aren't bothered. They just don't want to make out they're Pakistanis. They're not interested in their background or anything . . . They just want to be themselves, just like eveybody else." (Pakistani girl)

It is important to bear in mind issues of gender roles, personal identity, and cultural values as we explore teachers' and pupils' views of group work in the classroom.

A cautionary note: in talking to pupils and teachers about group work we did not over-emphasize the multi-ethnic context lest we distort the pattern of perception. In presenting the responses, we give weight to comments that do not relate specifically to the multi-ethnic population as well as comments that do. At the same time we are aware that one of the reasons why teachers in the school favour group work is that they believe it may – as much research would suggest – contribute to critical understanding and respect.

How do the teachers talk about group work?

"I'm fortunate in this department. No-one feels threatened by group work."

The English teachers are all aware of the benefits which come from co-operative learning methods in developing the language and communication abilities of their pupils. One teacher sees group work as playing an important part in the socialisation process:

"I've always felt when I have done it that the atmosphere in the classroom amongst the pupils has been improved."

He is worried by the aggression which colours the everyday interactions of pupils, in and out of class:

"It's not of a physical nature but just the way that they actually converse with one another."

"They say it's only play but I find it unpleasant . . . It's big and sort of macho, but the girls are just as bad as the boys. Anyway, I think that group work sort of breaks this down."

The aggression, he suggests, masks an inner insecurity which group work may trigger because group work itself can be threatening:

"A lot of pupils are very reticent about giving an opinion because they're terrified of it not being the right one. Also, . . . how will it be received by peers. Will they be berated for being a swot or will they be laughed at?"

In the past some teachers adopted a tough manner:

"There has been this sort of macho image. You know, 'Talk to me again like that, lad, and I'll smash your face in'. But I don't think you get so much of that now. Well, you can't because they know it's only bluff!"

But English is seen as a discipline in which language has a key role to play. Another teacher explains:

"They are exploring how to use language in the different language registers, something that I've always considered to be such an important part of the lesson – the fact that they should be discussing things with each other first of all before they even attempt to write anything down."

Talking, in her view, is a way of ensuring that pupils are thinking:

"If one makes a point the others can pick up on it whereas if the teacher's just standing at the front . . . they don't seem to be thinking or even participating themselves in the lesson."

"The ability to express oneself orally, to state a case, to argue a case, to justify the point, I mean all the things that we as English teachers hope that we can get our youngsters to do."

Group discussion, according to another teacher, should result in a greater depth of learning:

"I think you get far more active involvement in the learning when there is the interaction in the group. I mean even down to the most basic level where they can actually converse in their own groups about whatever has been said in the language of instruction. In their groups they turn it into their own language to grasp the concept."

One teacher rates the ability to *listen* especially highly:

"I think it's the most important thing because most of our kids are great at saying what they think but they don't listen to each other, they don't let each other finish speaking. So they never have time to weigh up actually what the argument's about because they're so busy thinking in their minds what they're going to say next or just shouting it out."

This teacher also justified opportunity for talk in school in terms of a relative absence of talk in pupils' homes:

"I don't mind if when we start group work it falls into a natural conversation because often they don't get the chance to talk much at home."

"This is generalising but, you know, telly goes on, and for a lot of the Asian girls they've cooking or looking after the kids all night, while the boys are at the Mosque. For a lot of the other kids, a lot of the parents work at night. So for many they don't see their parents because by the time they get home they've just gone out for the night shift and as they get in they go off to school, so there's very little talking."

The same teacher also sees group work as a means of helping young people from different cultural backgrounds to share experiences:

"At least once a month we just sit and talk. And I learn more in that time. It's very important, and not about anything. I mean we'll start off . . . The other day I got the newspapers of the day. The idea was to compare the newspapers and the reports but obviously the kids weren't up to that and in the end we just started talking . . . Most of these kids have very hard lives. It's nothing like we've experienced, and they've got to put it into some sort of perspective in their own minds."

Thus, through the informal exchanges which occur during group work the pupils might also extend their ability to understand and appreciate the perspective of others. This is particularly important when all classes contain young people from a variety of backgrounds. One teacher saw group work as being useful in attempting to change prejudiced attitudes, though she would have liked more expertise in knowing how to harness this potential.

Another teacher put it this way:

"They will learn about other people's attitudes which they will never learn by putting something down in writing and then all 20 of them handing that in to me because generally they only informally get to read one another's work. Obviously within our setting perhaps with a good ethnic mixture within the group, they'll learn an awful lot about people's traditions, home life and so on and they'll learn that better in group discussion than they would in class discussion."

The composition of groups: some dilemmas

How are small groups formed? One approach is to keep the pupils in friendship groups:

"I prefer people in friendship groups which often means that groups may not be the same size. I would even tolerate a pairing or two."

This approach is based on the premise that the individuals within a group need to have some common ground if they are to work effectively:

"I feel that it is important to get a sort of philosophy of the group established first before we start. There is no point in causing problems in the classroom by trying to make certain pupils work together when they're not friends or they don't get on."

But it is also, as the teacher acknowledges, to avoid trouble. At the same time, the teacher is not totally happy about groupings that result from free choice:

"This lesson is odd in the sense that out of 23 pupils we've got 14 or 15 Asian girls, so the people who are likely to want to be together are the white kids because there's so few of them. I think we've got one pairing of an Asian girl and a white girl. And there's one pairing of a white boy and a white girl . . . It may be that because there's so few of them that they're prepared to cross the gender barrier rather than the ethnic barrier."

Another teacher outlines the problem:

"Usually I leave it to friendship. I suppose I feel guilty that I haven't got mixed gender groups in there. What I've done in the past is to get them to work in pairs first of all so that they are with a friend and that gives them a bit more confidence, and then I say, 'Right, pair 2 you're going to work with them'. And that has been quite good but the only thing I find with that is that I can't get the Asian girls to work with anyone other than 2 other Asian girls."

"It's amazing! Some of them run across the room to find a pair of the same sex, and I find that so frustrating. But then I find that I don't want a fit of the sulks from any of them. Perhaps I ought to handle it better".

She suggests that cultural pressures place constraints on the Asian girls:

"They're not expected to work alongside (boys). It's frowned upon I think. They don't seem to have a lot of freedom to do things and that worries me."

Another teacher finds that splitting up friendship groups has a bad effect on the pupils' work:

"At first I thought they're second years so they won't know each other so I'll move them about. I don't want them to sit with their friends. We'll have five different groups. So again I did this numbers thing and it was a complete disaster because they were with people whom they weren't used to communicating with and who weren't on the same wave length. The people they had already chosen were already people of like minds."

This teacher is also aware of the need to be sensitive to the feelings of young people who do not have a friendship group with which to be affiliated:

"I do tend to let them go off in friendship groups and then you always have one or two left over that you have to gently or forcibly push into a group somewhere."

Another teacher is aware of the tension between achieving a mixed gender group and achieving a group that will work productively together:

"With experience you get to notice if there are three or four girls who will join a group of boys if you ask them to, but they work far better if they're working on their own or in their own friendship groups rather than having a male presence."

And he gives another example where intrusion by the teacher would have been inappropriate:

"In the present GCSE drama group there are three Pakistani girls who have opted to do examination Drama. Now before in the school I've only ever had one Pakistani girl come through a couple of years ago. . . . They're still prepared to join a full group but planning-wise they prefer to work in their own little island. They're quite prepared to show what they've done to the rest of the group and to have the rest of the group comment on it ... I'm quite happy with that." (T13)

In fact, one year later, the three Pakistani girls now have the confidence to work consistently with two other girls, one white and one Somali, and with this support are now contributing to a full group production - an outcome which the teacher himself admits he could not have predicted. He gives another example of a situation in which he felt he was justified in supporting boys working together:

"With two boys, their work is really just like a Marvel comic and so they made it work because they knew the Marvel comic language whereas with a boy and a girl it just wouldn't have worked at all."

Not only do teachers have to take into account the feelings of pupils about the composition of work groups but also the implications of different 'mixes' for overall class contact:

"Usually for group work to work you need to split up the noisy ones, the lively ones, and that means that some of the more serious ones get them in their group and they get fed up with them. They think: 'Oh, she's experimenting with that again. She's making us talk again. That means we've got to work with so-and-so, and that probably builds up, every time, against it."

The pupils themselves seem to be aware of the importance of their personality differences:

"I don't think that the quiet ones appreciate that there's anything to be gained from working with a noisier person. The noisy ones do appreciate it. It's like a little haven every now and again where they have to come away from their noisy friend whom they always have to be sparring with - if you *can* get them physically away from each other, preferably with some actual physical division between them, so they can't even see one another, then they stop worrying about what the other one's doing and what

the other one's thinking and they will get on with some quite
good work and in the end they will say 'That was good.
I enjoyed that'. So in the end they enjoy it though they wouldn't
actually choose to work with someone they don't know very
well."

However, one teacher suggested that by the fourth and
fifth year some barriers were breaking down:

"In my fifth year English group the Asian girls and boys sort of
sit together really . . . It's not to do with relationships outside school.
I think they're mature enough to sit with someone that they actually
like working with."

Sometimes new links are formed because pupils work
together on summer holiday jobs and the links continue in
school.

Perspectives from different cultures

"If someone comes out in the group with some statement that you
find very offensive then you've got to handle it there and then
and that goes back to the structure. You're not in control of what their
response is necessarily going to be and you may come up against a
response that you hadn't expected or maybe you have expected but
didn't expect to hear it so forcefully."

Teachers expressed anxieties about the difficulty of
striking a balance between allowing young people to express
an opinion and dealing with the reactions which strongly-held
views might evoke. The role of women in society, for example,
was a controversial issue. One teacher described her own mixed
feelings about restrictions imposed on Asian girls by their
families:

"Girls seems to be denied the right to do things that they
see other people around them do; at the same time I can respect
their ideals on what they value because they are very close
families and they do value certain things that should be valued. But
they seem so oppressive towards the girls."

She also felt angry at the 'air of resignation' with which
the Asian girls appeared to accept their lack of freedom. How
useful might group work be in bringing cultural differences out
into the open? One teacher outlined the conflicts which had
emerged for him during group discussion about men's attitudes
towards women:

"It was all to do with working, in fact, and things like:
Should a husband show a wife his pay packet? Should women go
out to work? He was very dogmatic about all those things. The
husband's pay packet was his own; women should stay at
home; housework and domestic jobs were the women's domain; men
did DIY and mended cars and women washed and sewed and cooked
and so on. He fell back on his religious beliefs all the time. You know
in the Koran it says that. It worked quite well because he expressed
his opinion and the rest of us disagreed, and he was happy to accept
that. And maybe just a little bit of that did rub off in the end."

He made a useful comparison with another discussion
where Asian pupils expressed their criticisms of an aspect of
Western culture – the celebration of Christmas:

"I remember talking last year with a fifth year group about
Christmas . . . The Asians cannot really see what Christmas means
to people here any more because it doesn't seem to have any
religious aspect to it at all . . . We couldn't justify it
because basically it's true. I mean their festivals are religious
and the majority of people believe in that and they conform and
worship and everything else . . . It made the others think about the
way they felt that we observed something that was supposed to be
part of our "religion" and yet most people do not observe it in that
way at all."

And when he reflected on the lesson later:

"It's only now I'm beginning to realise, two Asian girls did a
very good piece of writing about it, expressing the way they felt that a
Christian celebrated Christmas, looking out from their perspective,
looking in on us. It's only now that it occurred to me how much
may have rubbed off on other people about someone viewing it from
outside naturally making some kind of value judgement."

In a similar way he felt that the boy who expressed his
strong views on the woman's role may have gained from learning
that other perspectives exist:

"The other lads who were by no means particularly bright,
they also had the same attitudes as me and expressed it before I did.
I let them do it first and there was another Asian lad whose feelings
were not as strong. So you got a range of views and from within the
different cultures as well."

Finding a voice

"Teachers who attend to voice listen to the person in the piece." (Graves, 1983)

"It would be nice if the younger generation got saying things themselves. Many teenagers want to read about their times, what's happening around them, their worries." (Arab boy).

Teachers are aware of the improvement in the quality of writing which occurs when students are given the opportunity to write for a real audience. And a great deal has been written about the need to give young writers varied opportunities for communicating with an audience other than the teacher in the role of examiner (Britton, 1982; Emig, 1971; Graves, 1983). In contexts where the purpose of writing is less a means for testing than for communicating ideas which are personally meaningful, then it is more likely that the activity will contribute to the mental, social and emotional development of the pupil. It is also more likely that the writing will reflect the life of the writer, and capture the episode which is being written about and the context within which it happens.

In this example of the work of one of the English teachers, we explore some of the ways in which pupils can collaborate over the production of a magazine written for a readership of peers and write about topics which are of relevance to themselves. The task had two aims – to heighten pupils' critical awareness of the mass media, and to help them express some of their own ideas in a style which would be interesting to peers.

There were many issues to be handled with sensitivity. Did the young people feel that they were able to express their own points of view in the classroom? School clearly played an important part in the lives of these young people, but formal lessons did not necessarily provide the most facilitating framework. One boy put it eloquently:

"School is friendly. It is a place away from home where you can be with your own age group. You can play, you can talk, share secrets you don't want all the neighbours to know. When it comes to school, there are people from your own land that you can talk to about what you should do, what not to do, give advice. You can get together . . . But generally it happens in breaks. It is more of a trial in lessons, because they generally do

something else. You don't feel free in class, no matter if
you're talking about your traditions and that. You don't feel free
inside . . . You know, at school we aren't able to express our feelings."

The teacher was convinced that by working collaboratively on their own magazine the young people in the class
might find this freedom to explore their feelings about issues
which mattered to them. But before embarking on the magazine,
some ground work had to be covered. For example, groups, with
the help of a questionnaire designed by the teacher, carried out
a content analysis of a variety of popular teenage magazines
supplied by members of the class. A complementary exercise
gave a framework within which students could plan the content
of their own magazine. By sharing out responsibility for different
topics in the magazine, the pupils could overcome some of their
inhibitions about expressing themselves in writing.

In addition, pupils were asked to work together on the design of graphics for the magazine and the production of photographs, using members of the class as characters for a picture story. In their groups, they would have the opportunity to draft and redraft items for inclusion in the magazine; an editorial board of pupils would have a say in selecting the final pieces. Within the groups, pupils could draw on the range of skills – artistic, literary, humorous, role-playing, technical – which were needed for successful completion of the task. Word processers were to be used to produce a professional-looking magazine.

Careful structuring of the activity was, in the end, an effective strategy. As a result the pupils in their small groups were able to share perspectives on the issues which they themselves identified in the course of the exercise – the absence of ethnic minority characters in popular magazines, the lack of reference to multi-cultural issues, the wholly Western styles in fashion and beauty pages, the predominance of romantic, escapist stories, absence of real-life concerns, eg youth unemployment. The discovery of these ommissions for themselves influenced the content of their own magazine, even though in many ways it stayed close to the format of popular teenage magazines.

It is important to be aware of group processes if we are to understand responses made within the working groups. There were times of frustration and boredom; groups did not always gel; there were times when individuals did not seem involved in the group tasks. Yet by the end of the module, there was widespread enthusiasm and a feeling of achievement among the participants:

Hussein *It was really good. And we learned about using the computer.*

Wayne *The best thing was collaborating and working as a team. (Why?) It means you get on a lot faster and hear each others' points of view.*

Peter *We've been doing a story on racial unity – a cliff-hanger ending. A few lads get together – an Asian kid, a West Indian kid and a white kid. They've got a hut in the woods which they've cleared out to use. They've found this crane. They're trying to get it started. Then there's three other kids who think the crane is theirs. They're racist. And they've just kicked in the hut. That's the cliff-hanger ending. They buy a catapult ...*

Mark *We like the cliff-hanger ending because it's like a real-life story.*

Jamie *Yes. After reading the cliff-hanger, I don't like the love story. It all happens too quickly.*

Mark *Yes. The cliff-hanger is more real.*

As the teacher said, in evaluating the outcomes of the module:

"I was obviously very pleased by the end result and the sense of achievement which the pupils communicated to me. What was noticeable was the pleasure that the children of lesser ability took in being part of a team which successfully completed a task. As to the advertisements, I thought it was interesting that the group accepted a message advert (the anti-war one) put forward by Tony, a pupil who found small group peer relationships very difficult. It highlighted the fact that young people do have wider concerns than pop, fashion and sport.

I suppose the final benefits were that the work helped them to gel better as a large group, raised their self-esteem . . . "It's much better than the school magazine" . . . and they are still very keen to work in this way. Unfortunately, because of the constraints of examination work in the fourth and fifth year, work of this sort is only useful from the point of view of oral assessment as the written content could not be entered for GCSE as an individual pupil's work!"

His sensitive, non-intrusive involvement with the groups was a key factor in the success of this module. It meant, for example, that he was quick to help the pupils overcome difficulties as they arose. Initially he was concerned that pupils were treating his guide to content analysis as a work-sheet with right and wrong answers rather than as an open-ended exercise. He had written suggestions for some answers, like 'Are the characters happy, healthy, young?' Some pupils seemed to think that it was enough to answer 'Yes' or 'No', and he had to stress that these were only guidelines. The habit of dependence on the teacher is not one which is easily changed.

A further difficulty concerned the balance of power within the groups. Did all members have an equal chance of being heard? Since this exercise was specifically designed to enable young people to write about their own interests and views, this was an especially important question. For example: the questionnaire asked "Do stories in the magazines have a message?" In one group, Pauline, a very dominant, Afro-Caribbean girl, said immediately, "No, there's no message" and began to write that on the sheet. Louise (a white girl) said in a quiet voice "Perhaps it's 'Love Conquers All'"; this was nearly inaudible. When she repeated it, she was ignored. Pauline scored out her reply and inserted "Always be open about the one you love". There was no further discussion. Louise's voice had not been heard. The teacher felt strongly that the class needed the structure of the questionnaire to help them plan out their own magazine. A totally open-ended invitation to do so would have been threatening, and he was aware of the need to provide support while still creating an environment in which voices could begin to be heard.

One of the difficulties was that the groups were initially very compliant and would have readily produced a magazine which followed the *Jackie* format to the letter. The teacher gently guided them to a position where they could begin to question the content of popular magazines and ask how far they begin to meet the needs of young people:

"You've analysed a magazine aimed at girls. Consider if you were going to market a teenage magazine that would appeal to you and your friends. That means you have to include boys. It need not, e.g., just contain *romantic* stories."

Discussion surrounding the content of the class magazine initially kept very close to the questionnaire without challenging it or going beyond its recommendations.

One of the concerns in the English Department had been the difficulties which Asian girls experienced. Preparation of material for the magazine also highlighted this problem. For example, a group of Asian girls focused first on "English summer wear" and began to discuss "the kinds of clothes that 14-year-olds like to wear". The clothes which they described were quite different from the shawal and kameze which each girl was actually wearing herself. The teacher intervened to ask whether they had thought of writing about Asian clothes. After all, the magazine was for *their* class, *their* contemporaries, for *them*. They seemed at first quite surprised that their clothes should be of interest. There then followed a long, animated discussion about their own clothes such as the fashion points in the embroidery of a long graceful hand and the border of hand-sewn beads arranged

PAKISTANI CLOTHES

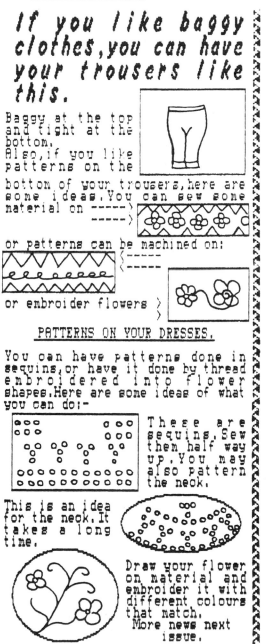

If you like baggy clothes, you can have your trousers like this.

Baggy at the top and tight at the bottom.
Also, if you like patterns on the bottom of your trousers, here are some ideas. You can sew some material on -----〉
-----〉

or patterns can be machined on:
〈-----
-----

or embroider flowers 〉

PATTERNS ON YOUR DRESSES.

You can have patterns done in sequins, or have it done by thread embroidered into flower shapes. Here are some ideas of what you can do:-

These are sequins. Sew them half way up. You may also pattern the neck.

This is an idea for the neck. It takes a long time.

Draw your flower on material and embroider it with different colours that match.
More news next issue.

97

in a traditional pattern. The result of this discussion was in fact a short entry in the fashion page on Asian dress.

Despite the teacher's repeated emphasis to the whole class that the magazine was "for black and white people, for boys and girls", unlike some of the magazines they had looked at, the Asian girls *still* thought that this would exclude their fashion. It took discussion in a small group for this possibility to be explored and for the Asian girls to be convinced. As Aenea, a member of this group, said:

"It's nice to know that someone's interested in our clothes."

It was clear to us as we observed and talked with these young people that they had enjoyed this experience of co-operative learning. Encounters with one another were friendly and animated; pupils generally worked well in friendship groups and in the groups arranged by the teacher. The pupils, in the course of producing their magazine, addressed themselves to controversial issues such as gender, personal identity and cultural values and, in the process, at least some of them showed their awareness of the potential use of co-operative group work in achieving the aims which we identified at the beginning of the case-study – understanding the perspectives of others, affirming one's own sense of identity, working in collaboration with others, discovering that the group can help each individual articulate needs and wishes.

We end with Wathek who, in evaluating the stories in the class magazine, illustrates with feeling how important this type of activity can be:

"Yes. There should be more stories like this. We do like "dream stories" (like the romance story) but also something of your own life, your own feelings. That's something you need. It makes you feel it is your own story. It makes you feel that I'm not the only one in the world who has similar problems . . . There are many kinds of people with feelings, thoughts, secrets they can tell each other. And if there was a page where they could – for different kinds of people – English, Jamaican, Arab, Pakistani, that would be a lot better. Because you could find out about your own life, your own feelings. And if they did get into that sort of situation, they'd realise that they're not the only one in the world like that."

THE POWER STATION GAME: A SIMULATION

In this classroom study we have an example of young people being placed in a situation where in order to complete a task it is essential to work co-operatively. In the space of two days, they must assimilate a mass of technical information, get to grips with controversial ideas, prepare and deliver a 30 minute presentation to an audience which will include peers, members of rival teams and a panel of experts in the field. What to most individuals would be impossible can be successfully accomplished in a group. This simulation had a very clear group goal – the presentation to an audience – and strong pressures on the participants to form a cohesive working group. The curriculum materials were well-planned and informative, and the challenging topic of discussion offered scope for controversy among participants. There was also the opportunity for young people to discover for themselves how co-operation with others can stimulate thinking and develop imaginative solutions to problems. The energy generated by collaboration can take participants far beyond the completion of the goal which has been set. There were rewards – both extrinsic and intrinsic – for performing well.

Although the game was originally designed for sixth-formers, the groups which we observed also included fourth-formers. We were interested to see how well a younger age-group would cope with the demands of this game. In the event the fourth-formers showed that they could cope very competently and that their struggle to be treated as equals by the sixth-formers offered an additional dimension to the task.

The Power Station Game

The Schools Liaison Service of the Institute of Electrical Engineering (IEE) has a keen interest in helping pupils understand what engineering is all about "without confusing them or making the subject appear outside their reach" (IEE, 1987). The IEE has found that one effective and interesting method of getting this message across to a wide audience of young people is to use the medium of engineering games.

The Power Station Game presents participants with a task – where to site a power station in a particular area bearing in mind the social, economic and geographical factors involved, and how to justify the use of coal, oil or nuclear fuel – which must be completed within two days. An engineer is available to give advice and answer questions. Their final design is presented in front of an audience and a panel of adjudicators who are experts in the field (eg in the finals (which we observed) the panel consisted of the Professor of Engineering from Sheffield University, the Principal of Sheffield Polytechnic and the Managing Director of Thorpe Hesley Power Station). The IEE also co-ordinates local media coverage of the event – press, TV, radio, SATRO Newsletter, careers bulletins – in order to give publicity to the Schools Liaison Service and to the schools.

Prizes are usually books on engineering topics to be used in the school library, as well as certificates for the pupils, and two trophies for winners of the final. In summary, the game allows:

- direct contact with head teachers and staff which facilitates co-operation between the IEE and schools;
- close contact with groups of fourth and fifth formers for two days;
- the opportunity to talk to other pupils about engineering during the event or at prizegiving;
- provision of books on engineering for the school library;
- publicity in the media concerning the IEE and its Schools Liaison Service.

Here's how one adviser from the IEE describes his role in guiding the pupils:

"The Power Station Game is a role-playing game in which we encourage students to examine the technical, the socio-economic and the environmental problems of building a power station in a particular area. We give them a pack which contains all the information they need to know. There are eight possible sites: all the relevant costs and all the technical information is there. Now until we actually give them the information on the morning that the game starts they've not seen it at all. So you can imagine that even sixth formers, and I would imagine even more so with fourth years, they've never done work like this and suddenly to have all this thrown at them, they're a bit overawed by it. What the IEE do is to try and put an engineer, an adviser, into each to steer them along. We're told quite categorically in the rules of the game that we can't do the work for them. But we can tell them if they're going in the

right direction or the wrong direction, and we can suggest to them different ways of doing the calculations."

How are the teams selected?

"There have to be at least three teams in a school because we give them three alternative fuels. We say there's coal, oil or nuclear. And the teams usually draw straws to see who gets which fuel. So they each draw straws and then get a fuel. Now having got the fuel they're then given the pack of information relevant to that fuel and they then drift away to their respective hideaways."

Once the three teams have been selected – oil, coal and nuclear – they are placed in separate rooms. This facilitates the way in which they organise their time and prepare their materials for the presentation, and creates an environment in which good communication among members can take place.

Co-operation and the resolution of conflict

We have seen that the Power Station Game has a clear-cut goal structure which requires co-operation amongst members of the group. There is no doubt in the engineer's mind that all the young people gain enormously from this co-operative learning experience. They move, in his view, from a state of confusion over the complexity of the information, which they must grasp, to an understanding of the social, economic and environmental issues involved in the siting of a power station. This achievement arises, he argues, to a large extent from the team work inherent in the exercise:

"I never fail to be amazed by the growth in stature of the participants. On the first day you see this look of horror on their faces. They think, 'Oh we'll never do this!'. By the end of the second day they are quite confident. By the time they get to the main final, they are very confident and self-assured if one compares with where they set off from."

How does this development take place? The presence of teachers or advisers is crucial in the initial stages:

"For the first half hour nobody moves; you can see absolute panic on their faces as they read through the information, and they look at each other and then either somebody will break the ice by coming and asking one of the advisers something, or we will go along and say can I help you and they'll give you a question. Once that's done, the adviser is kept busy because they come back with hundreds of questions."

101

The exercise is designed in such a way that individuals alone within the time limit could not handle the wide range of information or tackle the task of presenting their case to an audience. The advisers usually recommend that the groups break up into smaller working parties each with responsibility for a particular area eg statistics, graphics. From the outside it can look as if this process takes place with ease. As the engineer puts it:

"I'm amazed at how quickly they do seem to pick the right people for the right jobs. I suppose that's not unreasonable because they know each other very well, don't they?"

However, from the fourth-formers perspective, there were some problems to overcome before their contributions could be recognised as valuable:

"We were treated like slaves at first by the sixth formers. Doing graphics and stuff like that."

"Doing the graphics", which in the end played a central part in the effectiveness of the presentation, seems initially to have been perceived as low-status work. As one boy put it:

"The first day we were working in our groups. There was Amanda and someone else trying to work out what site we're gonna choose. Then there were two other people working out disadvantages for the others and for us, and then there were two other people getting the figures down, you know, how much it cost to run this, and then I was doing the graphics."

"The second day they *had* to use me so it was different because we only had a couple of hours to go. And then they were giving me things to do, so finally I did get some real work to do."

"Sixth-formers", said the fourth-formers in explanation, thought that "because they were older and doing more difficult things in education, that they were superior to us so we were given less important things to do". Fourth-form pupils could not assume that their work would necessarily be valued or even acknowledged by sixth-formers in the same team:

Pupil 1 *We didn't want them to take all the limelight, because we had done something as well, and it wasn't fair for them to take it all.*

Pupil 2 *Sixth-formers would be looking through stuff, coming and picking bits out of it, 'That's no good, you can't put that in, you can't put that!', and all that rubbish. I mean they were* *talking some right garbage, some people. (Laughter) They were though. They didn't know what they were on about. Like I'd got all these figures for the acid rain, I'd proved that our case was better, and yet one sixth-former said 'Can't have these figures', so then we'd got nothing. We just said 'Coal is better than oil', but we'd got no proof, and yet we'd got all these figures that could have pointed it out to them.*

Some researchers call this stage in the development of a learning group the *forming stage* (Johnson and Johnson, 1987, p.361) and describe it as a time of uncertainty when members try to find out the roles which they are to play in the group and the rules (both formal and informal) which control behaviour within the group.

The engineering adviser was aware of the formal rules of the game and perceived an easy transition from whole group dismay at the enormity of the task to well-selected sub-groups each working for the common good. From the inside perspective a different picture emerged. For example there were high-status tasks (eg preparing statistical analysis) which sixth-formers took by right; low-status tasks (eg illustrating arguments visually, colouring in bar-charts) were assigned to the younger age-group. The participants were in fact going through a normal stage in the development of a group as they sounded out one another's strengths and weaknesses and realised that they were all interdependent. These groups discovered that a task is more likely to be done well if all participants are motivated and feel valued, and found that the resolution of group conflict can be a productive force.

However, it must also be acknowledged that the response to conflict within teams varied. Some fourth-formers in the end were pushed aside and found the experience of taking part in the game an unrewarding one. They accepted the low-status roles assigned to them, obeyed orders and became uninvolved in the final presentation which for them had very little personal significance. By contrast, those who resisted the 'superiority' of the sixth-formers seem to have gained a great deal of confidence in their own ability:

M. *We sort of proved to them that we weren't stupid or anything, you know, we could actually work.*

F. *And they had to talk to us. The game was devised anyway*

*so that each member was dependent on the other so you had
to prove your worth because you knew that you were needed,
that the whole team should come together as one.*

P. *Half of the time we knew more stuff than they did. Only
thing they could do that we couldn't was some of the money
reading, because we didn't know the maths to work it out with.
When it comes to the arguments over it, a lot of the fourth years
knew more arguments than what they did.*

M. *It was worth it, you know, a good experience, we learnt
a lot of things, got on with people, things that you wouldn't
really do in normal lessons. It was worth having the two days
off I think to organise information, sort things out at home, just
basically find it out, do it, put it down.*

In fact, once they had overcome the barrier between
fourth and sixth forms, the benefits of group work were more
clearly seen. For one thing, motivation was very high. Teams
would meet up during the evening of the first day:

"Well, we started on the Tuesday and we took it home with
us and did something like three or four hours' work that night just
trying to get some acetates done."

Ideas developed out of team-work and graphics were
recognised as being extremely important as a communication
device:

"We got the owl idea. We saw that on a leaflet, and we
mentioned something about a circle round it using the acetate sheet
and Philip he improvised it and then we thought of the little wing and
things like that, so it gradually developed from there and we ended
up using it for the final presentation."

The wing, attached to the acetate sheet by a pin, could
be rotated to emphasise the six points which the speaker was
to make during the presentation. In that group, members had
realised the importance of trusting one another, of sharing ideas
and working collaboratively.

During the presentation to the audience, team work was
also essential. In fact, individualism, as members of one team
suggested, could be positively detrimental to the performance:

"The only thing we were let down with was the questions.
We had one girl, and she butted in before anyone else had a chance
to answer, like there was one section they asked a question on the
siting which me and another fourth year did, and we knew that on

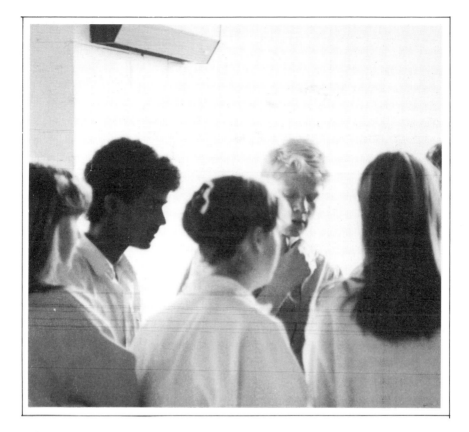

the site there was a proposed building site and an estate, and we knew about that, and she said 'Oh, we didn't know about that', so obviously we'd lost it just from that."

Some time spent in conferring with other members of the team would have given a truer picture of their thinking on the issue.

The presentation gave teams the opportunity to use one another as a resource when awkward questions were posed:

"In the final, we were conferring for a long time. Someone would ask a question and then people would all get into a group and confer."

And it was the support of the team which helped to calm nerves:

"You knew that whatever you said you'd have your team to back you up as well."

These are examples of a group with a strong sense of group identity where it is realised that all members are together, all participate and each one is inter-dependent on the other. The general opinions expressed by pupils, the teachers and the engineering advisers was that the team-work became an invaluable learning experience in its own right, whether the group won or not:

"It took us two days to learn all this about power stations, just two days! More discussion work in all our lessons would benefit us because if you go into the discussion work (and we don't really do that much) then everybody just thinks of it as a chance to chat rather than do the work, so maybe if we had more, then we would use the time, you know, to an advantage." (Pupil)

"I think actually it was a shame that some people only saw the presentation because to my mind it was the previous two days that were the most important. You know, sorting out your information, working together, getting it all together and deciding to agree on something. That was really more important than the end product." (Teacher)

The engineer drew parallels with the world of work:

"I think that one of the other things that perhaps comes out of these games is the fact that this is a sort of management training technique. It's a sort of leaderless group technique where you just put, six people together and say, 'Right there's a problem'."

Communication and presentation

The Power Station Game gives participants the opportunity to use their imagination and ingenuity to create stimulating visual aids which give the presentation maximum impact. They have 30 minutes in which to present their case and 15 minutes for responding to tough questioning by other teams as well as a panel of experts.

Pupils' emotions ran high before and during the presentation:

"Well, I really enjoyed it. I was a bit nervous sort of going in at first, sort of thinking what are we gonna do, how are we gonna get on, you know. But because we were so time pressed, you know, we really got on with it. It wasn't like you're thinking 'Oh well I've got a week and I'll leave it until the night before', you were really working. I really enjoyed it and I like getting the points over and people asking questions, and I like being able to answer the questions. It gave your ego a boost as well I think, actually. It gave you the opportunity, because I'm fairly outgoing, and I like to boast, I have got a big mouth, and it just gave people scope to show it off, you know what I mean, to put yourself forward."

For those who went on to the finals, the experience was challenging but also frightening:

"I did think though that it was extremely intimidating –
that impressive building and the room that we were in and the sort
of like Board of Examiners and it was like a do-or-die situation, if
you know what I mean."

However, the team-work which had gone into each stage of the preparation of materials gave individuals the confidence to stand up in front of an audience – making statements, producing evidence to back it and showing charts, slides, tapes, role-plays and other visual aids to support their argument. For example, one team arguing the case for coal used the image of a wolf to illustrate the dangers of nuclear power stations:

"There was a wolf going over Europe with a small nuclear
reactor. That was really complicated. It took most of the time up and
I think it was the best the first time we did it because we did it in
the school as well, and had the wolf with big claws like this looking
down and everybody sort of went OOH! like this when they saw it."

Balloons on a slide were used imaginatively to summarise key disadvantages in the use of oil-fired power stations. Then a balloon was burst at the end of the statement:

"THE CASE FOR OIL IS THEREFORE EXPLODED!"

The theme continued when a balloon containing flour was released to give the effect of radio-active gas. And the winning teams polished their presentations at each stage of the finals:

"They've had a lot of rehearsal and by the time the final
comes along the presentation usually changes considerably from the
school final. For example, the winning team this year put
letters from members of the public (concerned about the
siting of a Power Station in their area) up on an overhead and
simultaneously had a tape-recording of someone reading the letters
which I thought was an excellent idea. That was absolutely new to

the final. They hadn't used it in their school or in the LEA final."
(Engineer)

The pupils were highly aware of the importance of how you present your case:

"That was the whole point of why we used so much graphics
and visual aids because, I mean you really have to keep the interest
up, and it's awful sitting, watching something until you find it totally
boring. If it's something to look at you keep awake."

"Yes because I saw a lecture on television, an art lecture,
because my brothers like to watch everything to do with art, and this
man stood . . . in front of an audience, and he didn't put anything up
on the board, he was just talking for two hours, and it was so boring."

The emphasis on presentations was criticised, however, by one teacher who described it as "Razzmataz, this materialist approach to things prompted by the media," and she voiced concern that the *content* of the argument might be diminished in favour of a slick script:

"That's right. Now actually being asked to do that . . . I
mean you were asked to launder figures, weren't you, to try and
put your case. When you've been put into a position where you've
been asked to do that, of course it makes you more suspicious when
somebody else presents you . . . because you think ah well I've been
up to that." (Teacher)

The engineer disagreed:

"To say that they could get through with the wrong facts is
quite obviously nonsense because . . . what happens is they do
a good presentation. If the facts are wrong once the judges start
to ask them questions about their facts they become aware they've
got their facts wrong and that invariably destroys their self-assurance
which then loses them marks."

Yet it has to be acknowledged that in the heat of debate, some groups did consider distortion of the truth as a strategy for winning an argument. For example, one team had been told that there were plans to build a housing estate on the site which they had chosen for their power station. How could they cope with the criticism from opponents?

"We could have told a white lie and said 'They're not being
built now' but P. (a team member) butted in and said 'Oh, we didn't
know about that' and then contradicted herself and her argument
was all over the place."

Perhaps the experience of 'adjusting' information to support your own case and demolish your opponents can make you critical of 'facts and figures' in the mass media. This is an aspect of the Game which could profitably be explored during debriefing after the presentation.

Competition

We have looked at the experiences of individuals within each team, and some of the processes which are involved in creating a co-operative working group. In this section, we consider the competitive aspect of *The Power Station Game* and the paradox that at least some of the cohesiveness of particular teams grew out of inter-group rivalry amongst the advocates of coal, oil or nuclear power. The game proceeds through three stages as participants compete with teams in their own school, with teams from other schools in the LEA and, for the finalists, with teams from three other regions. At each stage there are winners and losers.

One danger of a competitive situation is that 'losers' become demoralised and no longer value their own efforts. This can cause members of the group to assign blame or to recriminate, thus undermining the cohesiveness which was built up in earlier stages of the game. The longer-term outcomes of the exercise may be lost.

How was competitiveness perceived by the pupils, teachers and engineering adviser? Opinions were divided. To some, competition is wrong, creates tensions, is damaging to both losers and winners and distorts the true purpose of the game. For example, the engineering adviser described discussion at a planning meeting:

"This year one or two of the Schools Curriculum Industry Partnership (SCIP) people said 'We don't think that you should have a winner. We don't even think you should have a trophy. We think you should just play it and not have any competition and just comment on how each team have done."

The engineer disagreed and argued for the positive benefits of competition as a preparation for the realities of life:

"Now I'm no educationalist. I mean I don't begin to be an educationalist, but to me that's sticking the head in the sand and I said so at the meeting and you know I don't see that you can protect young people from competition. Whether you like it or not that's what life's all about. When you start working you have a career, you are competing and the way you progress in your career is by competing against the next bloke. And I don't think it does any harm to expose them to a competition and to let them know they've done well, or equally that they've done badly. I mean how many times, in my career have I been in for a new job and I've come through a preliminary interview and I've been told I've been short listed and I've gone for a second interview and I've got on the final short list and arrived on the last day with half a dozen people, and I've still walked away at the end of the day without anything."

At this particular meeting a compromise was reached: there were winners and 'runners up' rather than a graded scale of teams (first, second, third, fourth . . .).

Some pupils' reactions confirmed the misgivings. Two girls were critical of the organisation of the game since it was not in their view clear what the criteria of good performance were:

"I think there should be a marking scheme . . . They told you there were lots of marks on presentation, but they didn't actually put the marks down on paper."

"For all we know, we might have got no marks at all for presentation and we might have been putting all this work into it and getting nothing out of it."

One finalist said gloomily:

"I don't know how we're going to explain to the Head why we haven't won the trophy."

Discussions with other team members, however, indicated that many participants found inter-group competition highly motivating and involving. Some described it in emotional terms. The competitiveness gives you "a feeling inside you", "it is enjoyable, it is really good", "I enjoyed it, especially when we beat them!"

They commented on the sheer fun of challenging other teams and scoring points off them. Some also argued that 'it kept standards high' since if people were not competing they would not try so hard.

The issue remains controversial. Among the pupils whom we interviewed (ie those who won a trophy at the final and those whose team was not selected) there was little evidence to suggest that inter-group competition had a negative effect on participants. Many said spontaneously that, although it was fun to compete with the other teams, it did not matter about winning since the game created an interesting experience in its own right.

We would suggest that one reason for this was that the young people understood quite clearly that the game was devised to heighten their understanding of an engineering problem, to develop strategies for coming to terms with new concepts and technical data, to develop skills in communicating and debating and, most importantly, to learn at first hand how to work co-operatively with other people. They saw the competitive structure as a vehicle to these ends and not as an end in itself. In fact, they used the game as a way of understanding another person's point of view by being forced to anticipate how a rival might argue or challenge.

One final aspect of *The Power Station Game* should be mentioned – the sheer enjoyment and vitality which was stimulated by the game at each stage. The game illustrates one productive way in which schools and industry can work together.

THE RESISTANCE SCANDAL: A ROLE PLAY IN SCIENCE

Background

The 13-14 year olds in form 3A were the top set for maths and English – but they also did science together. Girls outnumbered the boys and the majority view was that the combined science course they were following was a "switch off." We have good reason to believe that the normal teaching approach was in fact "good traditional." It was, we think, a combination of the image of science and the formal teaching approach that was generating some disaffection. The pupils were patient in their dismay, however, and not unruly.

One of their science teachers, Richard, had volunteered to join a team of teachers working at the Division of Education, University of Sheffield, to develop new teaching strategies in Biotechnology. Co-operative group work, using problem-solving and role-play approaches, was what they had focused on. Richard went back to his school, with other teachers in the team, to try out a small group, problem-solving approach (making methane) with 3A in a series of six double lessons. It went very well and the pupils talked enthusiastically about their first experience of problem-solving. All but one said that they had learned more and enjoyed their learning more when they were able to work in groups and to share their ideas and uncertainties:

"Well, we were given ideas and help but we weren't told exactly what to do. We had to use us brains. It were a bit scary when we first started but it weren't that bad. It weren't as hard as I thought. We did use our brains and work for a change."

"A teacher weren't there punching out facts to you and telling you, 'You've got to do this, and you've got to do that'. They just said 'Get on with it and work things out for yourself'."

"Yeah, and you felt better for it 'cause in the end, when like your experiments worked and you got the right conclusions that *you* thought of, you felt better for it, because you'd done it, and your teacher hadn't told you what to do, so really it was your own achievement."

"If you'd come in and showed us on t'board there's really no point for us to believe you. We haven't found it out for ourselves, but we can find it out and we've proved it ourselves. It's real. It's not something *you* just came in and did."

"Yeah, well, my friend, she's in a different science

class . . . and you had to copy it down in a book and she thought it was more fun finding out for yourselves . . . that it was more learning (but) it was fun. You'd want to learn it more than just writing it up from the board."

The one dissenting voice was Mike, a very high-achieving boy who was already doing maths with the sixth form. He said he had enjoyed the work, that it had made a "pleasant" change as a one-off, but he said he preferred it if regular lessons provided him with the facts. One of his classmates commented, very sympathetically:

"If Mike wants to be a scientist, then this (ie problem-solving in groups) is really more real in a way. He's gonna be faced with problems like this. He's not gonna be given the facts all the time. He's gonna have to work them out for himself. It's not really good practice if he wants to be a scientist to just say 'Here are the facts'."

His teacher said that he found it difficult to co-operate with others and preferred to work by himself. Mike explained:

"When I get the problem ordered in my own mind I just go straight ahead – and anybody else I just start arguing with them . . . I like to work things out in my own sweet way – then it's my own fault if it goes wrong."

Mike had in fact spent a lot of his own time researching the methane problem, and he did bring in his evidence to share with his group. At the end of the topic he was asked whether he thought he had acquired as many facts as he would have done from the more practical lessons. He said, with good-humoured honesty:

"I think I did actually because looking at the literature and gleaning your own facts is like being able to look at the world and take your own knowledge from it."

The group work task was involving and enjoyable, but he didn't see that he had gained intellectually from the interaction – although members of his group thought that his presence had helped them. Such an acknowledgement might make Mike see some value in group work, but for him thinking is more satisfying when you are working alone.

Four months later, when Richard and the team returned to the school to try out role play as a way of handling a controversial issue in science, the pupils were still talking enthusiastically about their problem-solving lesson:

"I can remember things we did in that but I can't remember what we did last week in several lessons."

"I wish we did teaching like that all the time. It's more interesting and I seem to learn a lot more."

"I've never worked so hard all term as I did then because I had to do things for myself."

". . . I hate science full stop. And come to chemistry I just switch off, whereas with that, your mind were open thinking you're going to learn something new and you just get on with it. It were great. I enjoyed it."

The role play was tried out, therefore, with a group already quite excited about the new way of working.

What the role play was about

This is how the role play was outlined in a briefing sheet for the pupils who took part:

The Resistance Scandal is about antibiotic resistance. We all want cheap meat when we go to the supermarket. So farmers have been giving ANTIBIOTICS to their animals. This makes them grow faster. This makes meat cheaper for you and me. That seems OK. But there is a problem. Animals have bugs inside them, like SALMONELLA TYPHIMURIUM. When the farmer gives the antibiotics to his animals the SALMONELLA bug inside them sometimes turns into a SUPERBUG. SUPERBUGS CAN KILL PEOPLE. But first they have to get inside you. But that's easy. When we eat meat (which is animals) we eat the superbugs as well.

You will be one of the experts in the list below. Soon you will be invited to Midtown TV studios. They have a programme called *Science and You.* This week on the programme they want to tell viewers the facts about SUPERBUGS. So they have decided to invite two teams of experts, including you!"

Team 1 (the consumer perspective)
CARE the doctor at Stumley Road Hospital,
SCRIBER the journalist on the Biotech Bugle,
BRAIN the scientist at Brightone University,
LOOKER the inspector for the Pharmaceutical Society,
GUARD the consumer protection worker.

Team 2 (the farmer perspective)
BROWN the farmer at Viriden,
LAMB the vet at Midtown,
MAKE the animal feed manager,
SELL the supermarket executive,
BRIGHT the meat tester.

What You Have to Do: When you have got the notes on
your role you should read them carefully. They will help you
to know what to say on the *Science and You* programme. You
could try rehearsing it with someone in your team. There will
be two teams. You will be in either the CONSUMERS team or
the FARMERS team.

When you and your team are happy with your roles you
should read or listen to the *Irish Story* and the *Illegal Drugs
Story*. You should also read the *Antibiotics Story* (or watch the
Superbugs News Bulletin). These are what started to make MTV
worried. So they will ask you questions about things on these
programmes. Your team should decide before you go on TV what
you are going to say. **You must decide whether antibiotics
should be used on the farm or not.**

What you can't do: You can't make anything up. What
you say on TV must come from what you have read, heard and
seen. But how you say it is up to you. **Remember that farmers
and consumers should each try to convince the millions of
viewers that they are right. You've got to know what you are
talking about!**

Journalist and TV audience
In addition, one person will be the Television Journalist.
Instead of being on one side or the other you will be in the middle.
Your job will be to ask fair questions. You must try to get the
experts to tell the truth. *You must get the team to decide whether
antibiotics should be used on farms or not.* Other members of
the class can act as studio audience. You must read the evidence
that you are given and find some questions that you can ask
the panel.

This is the first part of the briefing notes for pupils. The
role play is designed to help pupils explore the controversial

issues surrounding the use of antibiotics as growth promoters of livestock in the agricultural industry. The controversies surrounding growth promotion antibiotics arise because their use may be linked to the rate at which antibiotic-resistant pathogens appear, and to the development of antibiotic hypersensitivity in some people.

The table below summarises the structure, sequence, and approximate timing for the whole activity.

The structure, sequence and time of the Resistance Scandal

Briefing	Discuss the overview of the issues; set the scene				5–10 mins
Action	1. All read notes on their own roles, sitting as teams:				5 mins
	Farmers (5 roles)	*TV Journalists* (1 role)	*Consumers* (5 roles)	*Audience*	
	2. All look at evidence in teams and prepare questions				40 mins
	3. Submit five questions to TV Journalist	Collect and read all ten questions Know the audience's concerns	Submit five questions to TV Journalist	Submit questions	5–10 mins
		Television debate on 'Science and You' programme			15 mins
Debriefing	Discussion of the experience				10–15 mins

The debriefing

In this short account we have not concentrated on the role play itself: we ask you to trust the teacher's judgment that it was amazingly lively and that pupils handled the issues with more gusto and sense than he had expected! We focus instead on the debriefing discussion – a crucial component of role play – where pupils were invited to talk about what it felt like to be taking part. This was, we must remember, an entirely novel experience for them in science. The two questions that the teacher tried to explore with the pupils in the debriefing were these:

• do pupils feel tension if they have to play a role where the perspective to be taken is different from their own? If so what is the effect of the tension?

• do the roles enable pupils to contribute more openly than when they speak in their own person?

Role play supports group work in the sense that it provides a realistic framework for the exploration of different perspectives on an issue. It offers 'a reason to talk'. The members of each 'team' share a broadly similar view of the issue but there are slants that reflect the particular positions of individuals. Thus, groups of pupils have to work together within a common framework that determines their *overall* attitude to the use of antibiotics but they have space in which to decide which are the most important questions for them as individuals.

The teacher leading the debriefing first asked what pupils thought of doing role play in school as part of their work in science. They responded by talking about the quality of learning:

"It's easier to remember things like that, cause you've been involved with it."

"Yeah, you learn more."

Yeah, we get a chance to express our own views, and I like that.

"Instead of just sitting there and listening to teacher telling you what to do and write it down in a book, and you're 'spose to revise it for your exams, you remember more if you've done it yourself, if you've took part yourself."

"Yeah, if we have a part to play, or views to express, then we put ourselves into that role and, while we're in it, we find out more about it ourselves."

The teacher then prompted the group to talk about role play and the experience of talking 'in role'. The pupils' responses throw some light on the tension between their own personal view and the adopted view, and about the way that the debate helped them to consider alternatives and not just to defend their own personal position:

Teacher So you're saying then you actually felt that you were in a role, you were not just being yourself but you were in some sort of a role?

Pupil *Yeah (general agreement).*

Teacher Well, I think I can speak for this team (the farmers). We didn't actually believe what we were fighting for, so we had to

117

forget our own views and just look at the information we had, and form the views in the general direction to defend the farmers . . .

Pupil *I don't believe that they should be allowed to put antibiotics in, but I did believe it when I were arguing about prices, price of chickens going up an' that . . .*

Pupil *It's like arguing with yourself, isn't it!*

One pupil acknowledged that the tension she felt had reduced her to silence – "I couldn't say 'owt." She too believed in the argument being put by the consumers but her role required her to speak for the farmers! The teacher then asked more pointedly whether the pupils felt that they had learned more about the different perspectives by virtue of having taken part in a role play:

Teacher Does anybody else feel a little like that . . . that there are two sides to it?

Pupil *Yeah (general agreement)*

Pupil *When we were given the material, I thought, 'Well, I'm on the consumers' side, we should not use antibiotics' – now, I'm still on that side, but not as dogmatically and I can understand the other side's point of view.*

Pupil *And when we were told about it, it were all one-sided, what you were telling us, 'cause you were telling us what it did, there were no point to the farmers, so while we were arguing we've been – it's suddenly understood, whilst they've got to make a living, so it's . . .*

Teacher So really it's more complicated than you thought it was to begin with?

Pupil *Yeah (general agreement).*

The teacher also asked whether playing a role was difficult – but the answer was a vociferous 'no':

Pupil *I think if you just had to be yourself, I think it would have been all one-sided, I think most people would have gone for the consumers and when you've got a role, you feel that you've got to do everything you can to defend yourself and say what you feel.*

Pupil *And like on Lynn's side (ie the farmers) there weren't, like I said, there weren't that many people, and there'd have been no debate 'cause everybody would have been on one side.*

Pupil *And it was easy to say – they (the roles) give you a position in society so you can say, 'Well, from research I've done, in all this time', you know, and you can make it sound more obvious,* *but when you're yourself you think 'Oh God, what have I done?, What?' It's much harder.*

Mike, incidentally, was a talkative and engaged participant and collaborated well. His inclination to argue in groups (see earlier) was now harnessed to good effect since he had an 'opposing team' to take on!

Comment

The role play itself was lively. The pupils – including Mike – were engaged. They were also (as the extract above shows) quite articulate in the de-briefing session.

One benefit of taking a role is that it enables the shy pupil to hide behind it and to forget his or her 'known' timidity. In a school setting where pupils often get labelled and where they often feel that they have to live up to that label roles can be very liberating. A pupil can see him or her self differently, and they can see each other differently and value each other differently. We think that Mike's classmates valued him more from having worked with him in a group or team, and yet were sympathetic to his preference for working alone on a regular basis.

We were also interested in the testimony the pupils offered about seeing and understanding different perspectives and in the way that their own view was modified and clarified through being exposed to other views. As they said, when you had to justify a view that was different from your own "it's like arguing with yourself" or "battling with yourself". We think it important to help young people feel confident in accepting that there are different views, that views are often expressive of a particular interest, that personal views may sometimes conflict with the public view that one's professional group requires one to maintain, and that personal views can be modified, without shame, in the light of evidence that offers new ways of looking at situations.

As we can see in *The Power Station Game* and in *The Resistance Scandal*, simulations and role plays, although needing to be meticulously prepared, are in the end events which are owned by the participants. This is their strength and they therefore represent an important component of curriculum developments that are designed to support active learning and pupil autonomy.

Notes

The material presented here is taken from the Biotechnology in Schools Project, based at the Division of Education, University of Sheffield, and coordinated by Jenny Henderson. It was funded by the MSC as part of the TRIST initiative. The Project Report (an A5 book and a videotape) is available from the Project Coordinator.

The role play was developed by Vic Lally, Gleadless Valley School, Matthews Lane, Sheffield, S8 8JS. Full details, including 'role profiles and evidence' are available from him.

REFERENCES

Britton, J.N. (1982) Spectator role and the beginnings of writing, In M. Nystrand (ed) *What Writers Know*. New York: Academic Press.

Bruner, J.S. (1986) *Actual Minds, Possible Worlds*, Cambridge, Mass.: Harvard University Press.

Co-operative Group Work Project (1986) *Interim Report*, University of Sheffield.

Critical Studies in Art Education Project (1982) *Occasional Publications*, Nos. 1 and 2. Schools Council, in conjunction with the Arts Council and the Crafts Council.

Emig, J. (1971) *The Composing Processes of Twelfth Graders*, Champain, Illinois: National Council of Teachers of English, Research Report 13.

Graves, D. H. (1983) *Writing: Teachers and Children at Work*, Exeter, N.H.: Heinemann.

Institute of Electrical Engineering (1987) *Schools Liaison Service Newsletter*, Issue No.11, 2.

Johnson, D.W. and Johnson R.T. (1985) Internal dynamics of co-operative learning groups. In R.E. Slavin (ed) *Learning to Co-operate: Co-operating to Learn*, New York: Plenum Press.

Johnson, D.W. and Johnson, R.T. (1987) *Joining Together*, Englewood Cliffs N.J.: Prentice-Hall International.

Sharan, S. (1985) Co-operative learning and the multi-ethnic classroom. In R.E. Slavin (ed) *Learning to Co-operate: Co-operating to Learn*, New York: Plenum Press.

Sharan, S., Kussell, P., Hertz-Lazarowitz, R., Bejarano, Y., Raviv, S. and Sharan, Y. (1985) Co-operative learning effects on ethnic relations and achievement in Israeli junior-high school classrooms. In R.E. Slavin (ed) *Learning to Co-operate: Co-operating to Learn*, New York: Plenum Press.

Sherif, M. and Sherif, C. (1956) *An Outline of Social Psychology*, New York: Harper and Brothers.

Slavin, R.E. (1983) *Co-operative Learning*, New York: Longman.